NOISIA

A Critical Vision Book

Trashfilm Roadshows

Johannes Schönherr

A Critical Vision Book
First published in 2002
by Headpress

Headpress/Critical Vision
PO Box 26
Manchester
M26 1PQ
Great Britain

Fax: +44 (0)161 796 1935
Email: info.headpress@telinco.co.uk
Web: www.headpress.com

Cover design: Walt Meaties
Cover main image: Silke Mayer
Front & back cover snapshots: Johannes Schönherr, Katrin Krahnstöver,
    Todd Phillips and Christian Karl
Photos on p 13: Katrin Krahnstöver and Christian Karl; p 117: Photo: Christian Karl

British Library Cataloguing in Publication Data
A catalogue record for this book is available from the British Library

1-900486-19-9

Contents

Foreword
by Jack Stevenson

I was living in Boston in 1990 when friends in New York City rang up to tell me a couple of German guys were heading in my direction with a sack of 16mm films. They'd been showing them at various odd places along the East Coast and wanted to do a Boston show. So I arranged a screening in a big second floor hallway of what was more-or-less an abandoned building. We got a good plug in the paper that mentioned Fassbinder, Herzog, *et al.*, and posed the question, 'What's new in German cinema?' They might better have asked, 'What's new at a booze-soaked party in Nuremberg?' which is where most of the films came from — being no less worthy for it. We got a full house and it went well.

One of the two Germans was a skinny long-haired fellow with round wire-frame spectacles. He looked a bit like you might imagine an eighteenth-century classical composer to look — apart from his fondness for army jackets, black shirts, scarves and heavy boots. That was Johannes Schönherr.

Born in Leipzig in 1961, a week before The Wall was built, he grew up in East German suburbia. At one point he was picked to be groomed as a champion swimmer, but he turned out to be such a hopeless and unmotivated athlete that the project collapsed. Later, as a sixteen-year-old, he attempted to escape to the West via Czechoslovakia but was caught and got three months in jail and a suspended sentence.

Through the rest of the seventies and early eighties he hitch-hiked around East Germany and various East Block countries when he wasn't hanging out with other disaffected, hard-partying Leipzig youth. All this led to a job as a gravedigger in 1982, which he remains adamant "was the best job in my life". Still, it didn't keep him in East Germany.

In 1983 he managed to get himself kicked out of East Germany and made his way to Nuremberg, in the western part of the country, where he lived with a loose cadre of punks in a squat building. He began to hitch-hike around Western Europe, went to Central America for half a year, and eventually enrolled in the university in Erlangen.

In 1985 he joined the 'Kino im KOMM' film collective in Nuremberg. He became active in programming their cinema and eventually embarked on his own film projects, such as organising tours of prints from The London Filmmakers co-op. He also ran a free mail-out service, collecting schedules from the various German off-cinemas and sending these packets back out to theatres across the country, thereby spreading ideas and programming possibilities. He used the copying and mailing facilities of the Kino im KOMM and the Nuremberg Film House — where he also now worked as a projectionist — to accomplish these mail-out intensive projects which would soon also include booking tours for film-makers. This set a pattern for his style of operation: working within these groups and using them to advance his own initiatives, initiatives which were clearly outside the boundaries — although certainly not the spirit — of these organisations.

In 1989 he began to make contacts with the underground film scene in America.

One night he met another cineaste named Gert Weidenfeld, and after what we might assume were a few beers, they decided to go over to the US the very next day and show films there. That's when I met him for the first time.

Soon after that original foray to America, he applied to and was accepted in the cinema studies department of New York University. He moved to the city and began something of an American chapter.

The esteemed, now deceased, film historian William K Everson was one of his teachers. At the traditional end-of-semester 'student request' film screening Everson held at his flat, Johannes asked him to show exploitation titles so obscure and far out that even the walking encyclopaedia Everson claimed he had never heard of them... or possibly only pretended as much, since by this point Johannes' taste in film ran to the extreme fringes of trash, exploitation and porn.

The couple of years he spent at NYU gave him a foothold in America. He got a chance to spend lots of time at his beloved Mars Bar on the Lower East Side, to improve his home-made English and to investigate the back alleys of the New York film scene, a milieu he wrote about for various publications, among them the Danish film Journal *Kosmorama*.

He also made film-related forays into other parts of the country, elaborated upon in the pages that follow.

I've kept in touch with him over the years, while we've both moved from place to place, following news of his continuing projects with, by turns, admiration and disbelief. And I've occasionally been involved, sometimes as an active accomplice and other times, quite happily, from a greater distance.

Over the years he's been able to merge his obsession for film with his wanderlust, creating something less than a career or a steady job and yet something considerably more: a chance to travel and to discover new films, cool scenes and meet strange people. Most of all, to expose unsuspecting audiences to his latest filmic obsessions.

There has been a lot of laborious paperwork of course, but he's been equal to the task, intrepidly organising vastly ambitious festivals and tours that would normally take an office full of people to implement. Not bad for a guy who has the shittiest hand-writing on the face of the earth. Conversely, his activities have at times been tinged with a hint of international intrigue. Like a poor man's James Bond, he has drifted through the seedy bars of Beijing, killing long days and nights awaiting his Visa to be approved so he may get to North Korea... he has found himself in the rougher parts of exotic European capitals, while waiting to meet 'the Japanese connection'... crashed obscenely well-catered parties at festivals from New York to Gothenburg to Berlin, and so on.

He has had encounters with the world of institutionalised, subsidised film culture and has occasionally worked within it as something of an independent contractor or, rather, a double agent, to accomplish his goals. (He worked for months in the Danish Film Institute's grand building in Copenhagen to realise his touring Japanese film series in 1998, literally locked into the offices at night where he haunted the computers, phones, fax lines and copy machines... living by day in a cheap hotel.) And yet the territory he has staked is clearly outside the 'official' terrain of film programming, a milieu populated by people who are working paid jobs, having endless meetings and arriving at bland collective decisions on film selection and context — decisions that so often lack obsession, edge and inspiration. He has remained fiercely and incurably independent from this world, to no benefit of his bank balance. You could call Johannes the ultimate renegade exhibitor. He's done everything from bar shows to major European festivals.

And what ultimately comes out of it all are stories. That's what the movies are supposed to be all about, right?

Introduction

Back in the 1980s, I had two favourite pastimes: hitchhiking around Western Europe and watching weird, far-out movies. My favourite movie house at the time was the 'Kino im KOMM' in Nuremberg, Germany, the city where I was living. It was a dingy space on the second floor of Germany's biggest independent youth centre. More often than not, it was necessary to fight one's way through crowds of punk rockers, junkies and all sorts of rebellious kids in order to reach the theatre. The projectionist at the Kino im KOMM would sell the tickets, sell the beer, voice extensively and at length his views on the movies playing before eventually starting the show (which was whenever the projectionist thought everyone who was going to arrive had arrived). The Kino im KOMM showed a lot of films I wanted to see: Italian neo-realist pictures, French new wave, New German Cinema, punk rock documentaries and the films of the nascent New York no-wave scene. However, there were many films I still felt were being left out, which is why, in March 1985, I joined the Kino im KOMM collective myself. The first film I included in my fresh capacity as programme scheduler was Leni Riefenstahl's *Triumph of the Will*. Although the film was shot in Nuremberg, no theatre in town dared to show it and even within the Kino im KOMM itself there was strong resistance against screening such "fascist propaganda". But the film is an important part of the history of the city — and the only noteworthy movie ever made there!

It took a few years to exhaust the German distribution channels, but I did arrive at a point where there were many films I wanted to show but which remained unavailable domestically. At the end of the eighties I made another career move. I got in contact with similar theatres around Germany and started to build up a network with the ambition of importing film prints from America and the UK, touring them through different cities while sharing the costs with the other cinemas. The first film to travel this circuit was a 35mm print of Conrad Rooks' *Chappaqua* which I imported for a few weeks from England.

In the autumn of 1990, I went to New York for the first time. Not wanting to be a mere tourist, I took with me a few Super-8 films that friends of mine had made, with the idea to perhaps arranging a few shows on the East Coast. It worked! Though the income off the shows' admission didn't nearly cover my costs, I had found a new and exciting way to travel: instead of hitching into some strange city late at night and not having much plan of what to do there, I would now get in contact with hospitable film people who would arrange a screening, allow me to stay in their homes, show me around town and introduce me to other interesting people — just as I had done with visiting filmmakers in Nuremberg. My hosts would always try to connect me with movie folks in other cities. I loved it! I went from New York to Washington DC, Philadelphia, Boston, and back to New York, connecting there with the 'Cinema of Transgression' scene.

Back in Europe, I soon went from shipping film prints around to arranging personal tours for American filmmakers. The first such tour had New York Cinema of Transgression filmmaker Richard Kern showing his work in twelve cities in Germany and Holland.

In 1992, I left Germany and moved to New York, only to re-open the film tour business shortly after: a friend back home coordinated the tours of European cinemas, while I scoured the New York underground scene for interesting talent.

But my main goal was to visit places myself and to introduce fresh audiences to films they would perhaps otherwise never have a chance to see. I got invited to places as varied as Copenhagen (which seemed to be the world capital of affluent underground movie connoisseurs in the early nineties), Budapest (where nobody had much of a clue what was going on onscreen), and Moscow (where they love all things bizarre). It got me into driving from coast to coast America. In 1997, I did a tour of Japan with an American underground film programme, showing the films in such places as a Rock club in Kyoto that was going out of business the very next day (not because of my movies, I might add!), the Nagoya art school, and the main hall of a Shinto Shrine in Fukuoka. I went back to Japan in 1999 to show vintage American porn from the 1920s. Such movies were strictly illegal in Japan because of a law that prohibits pubic hair onscreen — but who cares! In 1998, I took a large programme of Japanese underground features around Europe, travelling with the films and operating a softitler* at each cinema, since most of the films had no subtitles. I drove from town to town with the big subtitle display machine and all film prints stuffed into the back of a rental car, showing the films in places as diverse as Norway's State Film House in Oslo and the small independent Munich Werkstattkino.

The strangest place I ever went on movie business, though, was North Korea. I didn't go there to show films but to select a programme of North Korean films to be shown in Europe. They were not underground, of course — there is no underground film scene in North Korea; people would probably get shot on the spot for making something that didn't adhere to the politics of the Worker's Party. Rather, those movies were over-the-top propaganda from the most reclusive country in the world, from a country that feels more like the compound of a suicidal sect than a real country.

In early 2000, I could be seen driving around Europe again with prints and softitler in a rented car — this time confusing jaded cinephiles with whacked-out North Korean propaganda praising the Great Leader, glorifying peasant life in the "best country on Earth" and advocating war for the "independence of the whole world"...

*Softitlers are used mainly at film festivals in Southern Europe. These digital display boards are placed directly beneath the screen and, via a computer and timecode programme, provide subtitles for otherwise non-subtitled foreign language films. Subtitling a film is expensive; operating a softitler only requires that the subtitle text be typed into the computer and then placed in sync with the dialogue.

Trashfilm Roadshows is a collection of stories from those pretty strange, zero-budget movie tours. I hope you enjoy them.

Johannes Schönherr

Riot Cinema

Programming a high-brow art movie house and booking critically acclaimed masterpieces and pretentious oddities month after month, year after year, to appease a minuscule crowd of sober-minded cineastes and feeble-hearted intellectuals — what utter boredom! Cinema should be a place for excitement and adventure, for surprises, shocks, and troubling insights into the amazing world of the human mind-set. If the screen action happens to spill out into the auditorium — well, that's all the better!

    In the late eighties and early nineties, I worked as a freelance programmer for the Kino im KOMM in Nuremberg, Germany — a place on the top-floor of a twilight zone of post-punk urban madness called the 'KOMM'. Located just across from the Central Train Station, the KOMM — or Communication Centre, as was its official title, a huge mass of a building still visibly scarred by the bombs of WWII — had been set aside as a publicly funded playground for the city's misfits. The reasoning being that it was better to keep them there in the one place, under the observation of social workers, than to have them spread out all over the city. On one hand, the KOMM functioned as a dingy cultural centre, with several concert halls, an exhibition space, numerous bars, and the cinema; while on the other hand it was a secret bastion of leftist streetfighters, it's graffiti-strewn hallways populated by

Nick Zedd
A Cursed
Night in
Nuremberg

doped-out punk rockers, homeless winos, heroin zombies, and Turkish drug dealers.

To reach the cinema, one had to step over the semi-conscious lowlife sprawled across the slime-covered fake-marble stairs. Once inside the sanctuary of the cinema however, it was possible to relax, open a beer, light a cigarette, and engage in whatever excursion to the outer fringe of the mental landscape was unfolding up on the screen. Cinematic psycho killers, alien monsters, acid freaks and necrophiliacs played back-to-back with home-made Super-8 atrocities, sexploitation flicks, and wonderful works of the American underground.

Not all of which was met with universal approval. One faction of the KOMM followed the activities of the cinema with a deep suspicion — the leftist streetfighters. They regarded the KOMM as their revolutionary stomping ground and themselves as moral watchdogs presiding over the ideological purity of the place. A junkie puking on the floor — that was fine with them as they considered it an expression of the social misery of the underclass in the capitalist police state of Germany. Explicit sex on screen however, was intolerable; it was pornographic, sexist, misogynist — more than all of this, it was being projected under their very noses!

It was precisely this direction I was heading with my curating. Despite the fact that some of my cinema colleagues strongly opposed it, I

Typical scene in the KOMM hallway.

Next page: KOMM programme for January, 1990, announcing a Cinema of Transgression weekend. Two months prior to Nick Zedd's riotous personal appearance, the January show fired many emotions and lead to the attack in March.

felt compelled to throw more and more sexually explicit material into my programmes, and I announced them as such. Why not? Sex is as an important part of life as it is of cinema — so, up on screen with it!

It was in the Winter of 1990, a time of heated discussion on this very subject, that Uwe Hamm-Fürhölter of ArtwareProvision in Wiesbaden, organised a German tour for Nick Zedd — mastermind behind the New York Cinema of Transgression. I booked the show, and had no qualms about announcing it as a provocative and scandalous event. I even used the dreaded p-word, describing Zedd's film *Whoregasm* in the cinema

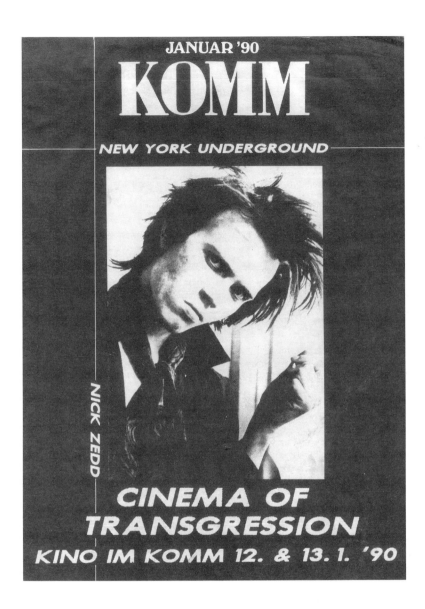

JANUAR '90

KOMM

NEW YORK UNDERGROUND

NICK ZEDD

CINEMA OF TRANSGRESSION
KINO IM KOMM 12. & 13. 1. '90

programme as a 'pornographic experimental film'. Furthermore, I wrote, the Cinema of Transgression had already caused *Fascho-Feministinnen* — fascist feminists — to wreak havoc at a cinema in Berlin.

I was playing with fire to create some excitement. And it didn't take long before copies of my programme notes found their way onto the walls throughout the KOMM, pasted up with the words 'pornographic' and 'fascist feminists' highlighted. Rumours began to circulate that the 'fascist feminists' — the radical feminist offshoot of the KOMM

streetfighter faction — were preparing to make a stand against this type of programming. Leftists had frequently announced action against the cinema in the past without following it through. I suspected the rumours in this instance would also amount to nothing.

On March 8, Nick Zedd arrived, accompanied by Uwe Hamm-Fürhölter, his tour manager. A pale redhead, Zedd was a pretty shy and anxious guy who put a lot of effort into hiding his vulnerability behind a 'Fuck you' attitude and arrogance.

I met my two guests at the door of the KOMM, navigating them through the stupor-gazing drug-derelicts and up to the cinema where we started to prepare the show. Zedd was travelling with his badly spliced Super-8 originals and was deeply worried that the films might get stuck in the projector gate. All the test-runs were fine. With the films threaded, their focus adjusted and the sound cued in (the audio coming from a tape played on a cassette player), we let the waiting audience in.

Well, my scandal-mongering had paid off — it was almost a sell-out crowd.

Taking a last glance through the projection booth window before setting off for the auditorium and introducing Zedd, we were confronted by the sight of maybe seven or eight people jumping up and down the aisles, blowing whistles, their faces covered by ski masks. "Hey, Uwe!" I yelled. "Get over here and take a look at this! It's great!" The black-clad protesters continued by throwing flyers into the air, eggs at the screen, and garbage and cat shit indiscriminately. Then they hastily left the cinema. The whole action was over in minutes. What a neat little introduction to the movies, I thought — but the only one not amused was Nick. He feared the worst. That perhaps the leftists would come back and beat him up, or something. There was no way to convince him otherwise, or to dismiss the protest in his eyes as being merely some extra — free — promotion for his show.

We went into the auditorium to face the somewhat bewildered crowd. "It appears we have just had a visit from activists," I said, "who wanted to give the place a design appropriate for the dirty movies you are about to watch." Nick went on to tell the audience that the "feminists were certainly no environmentalists" and that they wasted their energy on the wrong target.

If our impromptu speeches didn't help to enlighten the audience on what had happened, neither did the badly designed flyers the protesters left behind. Was it all a part of the show, planned by us beforehand, queried the audience, or were those whistling chicks protesting for real? (Weeks after the event I was still being asked this question.)

Expropriate speculators!
City pirates

One person who had no doubts about the veracity of the protest however, was Nick Zedd. He insisted for the duration of the show that he remain behind the locked fireproof steel door of the projection booth. We agreed, and from there studied one of the flyers deposited in the auditorium. The crusade was a blow against the 'reactionary chauvinist provocations of the stooges of the patriarchate in the cinema group' — me — who went so far as to stage a 'sexist show on March 8 —

International Women's Day'. Signed: 'Commando Lotte, Zora, Leila'.

We had no idea March 8 was a 'holiday'...

Somewhat grateful for the attention they had paid to the cinema's exploits, I toyed with the idea of going over to the Molotov Club bar within the KOMM — the major leftist hangout — to advise Lotte, Zora and Leila on when best next to hit. Good sense prevailed — probably sparing me a trip to the hospital — when I considered that interrupting their 'victory' party perhaps wasn't such a bright idea.

(Not enough sense to stop me attending an 'anti-imperialist' party a few days later, however, where — regarded by everyone as a 'porno pig' — I ended up in a fist-fight.)

Nuremberg: Protest against Sex Films — Women throw Garbage Into Cinema.

Newspaper headline on the leftist attack at Zedd's show.

After cleaning the cinema of its garbage, along with a futile attempt to clean the egg stains from the screen, we left the KOMM — much to Nick's relief. But Nuremberg had more horrors in store for our transatlantic visitor. Stopping off at a bar, a dark space inhabited by art students and local hipsters, I made out the faces of some well-known KOMM-based leftists. It was then that somebody who had been playing around with a canister of teargas managed to break off its nozzle. Gas exploded into the room, quickly filling the place and biting into eyes and noses. People poured out of the exit and into the courtyard, where the rumour started to circulate it had been an attack against Nick. Whether or not this was the case, we decided it was probably best to split anyway.

With a few hangers-on, we drove to my flat — the safest place in town, or I thought. After all, Nick hadn't anticipated a night of horrors. He was a visiting filmmaker who wanted nothing more than cash and the adoring attention of girls. The first he got; the latter not so much. And the night remained cursed.

One of our party slammed the main door behind us as we entered my tenement building. The commotion awoke the inhabitant of a nearby flat, a schizo who burst out of his smelly, trash-filled hole of an apartment and raced up to me. "That main door! I told you before!" He screamed, grabbing me by the throat. I caught a fleeting glimpse of seventies style pin-up girls adorning the interior of his apartment. Then, with Nick looking on in astonishment, we wrestled for a while — until I was able to unlock the bum's grip and proceed upstairs.

We had hardly poured our second drink when my doorbell rang. I was greeted by the sight of two policemen, who had been called out by my attacker downstairs. I told them the story and they left without any further ado.

The doorbell rang again. Evidently not satisfied with the indifferent reaction of the police to his complaint, it was the guy from downstairs again, dressed in his pyjamas. He started yelling. Curious as to what was going on, Nick came to the door. "What's he saying?" he asked me, and I started to translate my angry neighbour's outburst — which succeeded in enraging him even more. "Speak German! We are in Germany!" was his reaction. Which I dutifully relayed to Nick in English.

Then, suddenly, Nick exploded. The day had been too much and Nick's resolution to all the shitty events was an outburst against the screaming man at my front door. He jumped through the door, knocked the guy to the floor, and launched into a tirade — "Asshole!... Motherfucker!... Son of a bitch!" — before kicking him all the way back down the stairs. Finally, the face of the Nick Zedd I knew from the movies had emerged!

Of course, the incident resulted in a second visit from the police. This time, two particularly friendly young cops arrived, who declared: "Yes, we know the guy from downstairs. He's nuts." Nonetheless, they demanded Nick's passport. Perusing its pages, they then proceeded to address him as "Mr Harding" — much to his chagrin and embarrassment, as he evidently expected us all to believe that 'Nick Zedd' was his real name.

The next morning, I was awoken by the telephone. It was a journalist from Nuremberg's main tabloid wanting to know more about the incident with the KOMM feminists of the night before.

Beaming from newspaper vending boxes all over town, 'SEX FILMS: WOMEN ATTACK CINEMA' was the front-page headline the following day.

Thanks, you feminists. Hope you are back soon. And best regards from Nick — he loves your action... now that he is out of town.

Richard Kern publicity shot.

Next page: Kern tour poster, 1991.

Richard Kern The Bleeding Screen

A year after Nick Zedd's visit to Nuremberg, I myself got involved with organising personal tours for visiting American underground filmmakers. In April and May of 1991, I could be found driving Richard Kern around Germany, working as his tour manager. Kern's films, especially *Fingered* which he shot in 1986 in collaboration with Lydia Lunch, had caused uproar in Berlin a few years earlier. Its screening at the 1988 Berlin Film Festival had been interrupted by festival head Moritz de Hadeln, who chose to distance himself from the presentation of what he regarded "a vile and violent underground movie". Some weeks after this incident, when *Fingered* played the Berlin Eiszeit Cinema, feminist radicals broke into the theatre, smashed the projector, stole the box office takings, and poured paint over a film print, mistakenly believing it to be *Fingered*.

Now, in 1991, everybody remained calm. Kern and I drove from town to town, from cinema to cinema, without incident, projecting his two programmes of short films and having brief discussions with each audience. Not even the notorious leftists at the KOMM in Nuremberg crawled out of their holes.

Or rather, without incident until Mainz University... I had called ahead to arrange our arrival. "We've got a problem here," said Christian, one of the local managers. "You see, Volker and me booked the show in our capacity as event curators for the ASTA (Allgemeiner Studenten-Ausschuss*) at Mainz University." Christian continued: "The trouble started when we announced the programme in the student paper. The leftists and the feminists went nuts. They labelled the texts and film descriptions as 'sexist' and 'misogynist' — you know these

*The general student organisation common to every German university.

folks and their vocabulary. They called a big ASTA meeting, which they dominated. Volker and me got fired as curators."

"Are you saying the show is cancelled?" I asked.

"No, of course not," he replied. "It's gonna be held in the same space on campus as originally intended, except now it's officially a private event. The ASTA has nothing to do with it anymore." Christian paused. "Well, they still pay. I told their cashier it would be cheaper for them to come up with the payment than it would be if you sued them for breach of contract."

How nice of him. So where was the problem?

"Naturally, the feminists don't like the idea of the show going ahead anyway. They might try to interrupt it." "Sounds like fun to me."

When I related the news to Richard, he just asked: "You sure they'll pay? Then let's go."

Annabelle Davies in Richard Kern's film *Nazi*.

Next page: Flyer for Kern video compilation released in the US in the early nineties by Film Threat.

The campus of Mainz University is a large sprawl of futuristic looking concrete buildings. When we arrived, Christian and Volker showed us the posters our opponents had plastered all over the place, attempting to create confusion by erroneously stating the show had been relocated to a building at the other end of the huge campus.

The entrance hall to the auditorium in which the show was being held was literally covered with derogatory graffiti against its performance, combined with the bogus location posters. The latter I tore down, while Richard prepared the portable Super-8 projector in the auditorium. It was quite an academic setting: a huge glass-fibre screen behind a professor's desk, and ascending rows of writing tables for our audience. The projector was propped on a table at the rear. No steel door this time, or projection booth — we would be at one with the audience and open to any possible attack.

People came in and took their places, while many more remained in the hallway — protesters against the show as it turned out, who brandished well-worn accusations on cardboard picket-signs around their

HARDCORE

THE FILMS OF RICHARD KERN

necks. They remained in silence, quite prepared to simply display their message. Most were men — bearded pimple-faced hippie types who probably thought that such activism might help lubricate their way into a few female protester pants.

I talked to some of them. No, they hadn't seen any of the films and weren't interested in doing so, either. The propaganda they had heard and read about was reason enough for them to take a stand, they said.

"I would understand your refusal to check the films if you first had to pay to see them," I said. "But that's not the case here. The show is free. No admission. We get paid the same amount whether two people or 200 people show up. Why don't you give it a shot? You can always leave."

No, no, it wasn't about money, it was an issue of principles. "No violence against women on a campus screen," they argued. "Well, you are probably referring to *Fingered*," I deduced. "But that film is written by a woman who also plays her own violent role in it. It's actually violence by women we are showing here tonight..."

A lot of people actually got misled by the disinformation presented in the posters distributed by the protesters. But a happy Christian arrived with about 100 people in tow, plucked from the phoney location. The show could start! After a short introduction by Richard Kern, *You Killed Me First* began to play — a film in which Lung Leg, as a mentally tortured daughter, takes a gun and splatters the brains of her movie parents David Wojnarowicz and Karen Finley at the dinner table. *Submit To Me* followed, featuring the gory sex and death fantasies of numerous East Village underground luminaries. The show continued with more recent short pieces like *Nazi* and *Catholic*, wherein young girls take their clothes off in a playful way.

Then *Fingered*, the dreaded scandal movie. The film commences with the somewhat ironic introduction that

This film is an EXERCISE in the CAPITALIZATION
of an EXPLOITATION that some may find
unnecessarily VIOLENT, SEXIST
and DISGUSTING...

No sooner had the warning flashed across the screen when a group of hooded people ran screaming into the darkened auditorium. They circled the place, throwing flyers over the audience and bags of red paint at the screen.

As quickly as they had appeared they were gone.

They could easily have come up to Richard and I projecting the film and really interrupted the show, but they didn't. After their little intermezzo we didn't even turn on the lights. And the red paint on the screen — big jagged blotches spiked violently in all directions, from which slender threads rolled slowly out of sight — looked like blood over the black-and-white images of the film. Blood over Marty Nation as he jerked off while on the phone; blood over Nation and Lydia Lunch as they furiously fucked; blood over Nation cutting the throat of some guy making stupid remarks about Lunch; blood over Lunch and Nation beating up and then trying to rape Lung Leg, the desperate hitchhiker.

Driven by the furious desires of its main protagonists, the rough editing, and Jim Thirlwell's harsh soundtrack, the creeping red paint added an hitherto unprecedented dimension to the film. It was as if the white canvas of the screen alone couldn't bear the pictures projected onto it, the violent impact manifesting in a crimson ooze.

"The film should *always* been shown this way," I told Richard and he happily agreed.

After the screening, Richard and I were the only around to pick up the flyers. We kept as many as we could — souvenirs of a great show. The next morning we departed Mainz for more conventional, but certainly less memorable shows.

We defend ourselves! Here, violence is glorified under the guise of art! Your voyeurism stinks to the sky!

Feminist flyer from the attack on Kern's show at Mainz University, 1991.

Moscow 1992
Trashfilm Emissaries

"Nem," said the pallid shopkeeper on fancy Vaci Utca. "Nem," said the skinny old man in his mouldy stationary store a few blocks down the riverside.

Jack Stevenson, the San Franciscan trash movie collector, and myself, his European tour manager, zigzagged through the dreary, exhaust-fumed streets of slowly awakening Budapest. We were on a search for a product we had hitherto always taken for granted: liquid paper. Here we were in post-communist Hungary, with its new pizza parlours, burger joints, fancy Western clothes stores on every second corner — all around were the signs of a rapidly encroaching Western world, and yet as deficient as always were the basics.

No liquid paper.

Down lanes dotted with noisy tourist street cafés and through seemingly endless passageways undergoing some form of construction work, we dashed. Time was running out for the absurd enterprise we had in mind: in our pockets were photocopied invitations to Russia, issued to — who knows? These we planned to turn into blanks, issue to ourselves, and use to get hold of visas. Being Friday and the Embassy due to close for the weekend, we had less than three hours. By Monday night, we wanted to be feasting on caviar and vodka as celebrated trash film guests in Moscow.

Downtown Moscow.
Photo: Michael Zettler

As directed by a paper merchant, as ancient and as decrepit as a living being can possibly get, we dropped into a smog blackened side street with empty windows, then made a right onto Andras Utca. This tree-lined boulevard of monumental buildings from the Austrian empire days, still bore its communist name on street signs, Nepköztarsasag Utca — albeit crossed out with red bars. And there, finally, we had it — a humble department store with dusty cardboard flowers in the windows. Lead pencils, writing pads, office clips... Ha! A few bottles of the precious, German-made, Tip Ex liquid paper! The morning suddenly began to look a whole lot brighter.

Squeezed between pensioners reading newspapers, we sat ourselves on a park bench and started to obliterate the hand-written entries on our forms. Carefully, letter by letter, against the grip of the wind, we slowly removed the details of the original applicants. With this task eventually accomplished, we faced another: finding a copy machine. Back to the tired avenues, over which the remnants of a decades-gone glory hovered still. "Nem, nem," was again the overwhelming response in our quest. Photo shops: "Nem." Paper stores: "Nem." Perfumed hotel receptionists: "Nem." No one wanted to help two frantic document forgers lost in an Eastern capital.

Then came salvation in the form of a brand new Kodak store set in steel, glass and marble. Price was fifteen forints per print. A young clerk fumbled with the machine. Making a copy on both sides of the same sheet of paper was an exacting task. Head to toe on the front side, toe to head on the back. How could that happen? Another attempt, but the same result in reverse.

He could manage himself, he insisted. He didn't need any help.

The duplicates, when finally he got them right, looked no more than the crude facsimiles they were, replete with unconvincing stamp and signature. Anyway, onwards to the Russian Embassy waiting room. Dirty, noisy and panelled with brown wood like every Eastern room designed for public use, it was here we met our helping hand. His name was Laszlo, a young, black-haired Hungarian Russian-language teacher. Ex-teacher, to be precise — the need for Russian teachers in Hungary had diminished quite a bit in the last few years. With a fat-nibbed felt pen, Laszlo entered in Russian our personal data onto the forms we had spent all morning creating. After this all we could do was wait in line, slowly edging our way up to the wood-framed window attended by a grim-faced Russian officer in an unmarked uniform. There were no flags, or Soviet signs. The Soviet Union had broken up the year before. There were no Russian ones, either — Russia had more pressing problems than to spend time redecorating its foreign visa waiting rooms. In a hushed tone, Laszlo translated some of the stories he was picking up from people ahead of us in queue. "I wanted to go to Kiev a few months ago," one person commented. "That's Ukraine now — so I got a Ukrainian visa. But the flight went through Moscow and in Moscow I had to change from one airport to the other for my connecting flight. These Russian immigration guys tell me I can't go to the other airport because I have no Russian visa and cannot enter Russia — not even for a simple transit bus ride! A few months ago, all that was still one country! Do you know what they told me? 'Don't come here if you want to go to the damn Ukrainian secessionists!'"

We moved closer to the window. All this waiting was a complete turnaround of the hectic morning we had spent getting here. By now

The author (left) and Jack Stevenson at Moscow university, 1992. The poster says 'Taboo Films'. *Photo: Michael Zettler*

we were close enough to the window to hear the conversations between the bitter-looking officer and the other applicants. "No invitation from Russia?" he snorted at one man. "You've got to go with an organised travel group. Go to a travel agency, they will sort it out for you."

"But I'm a German businessman," responded the applicant. "I want to visit Russia on my own to explore investment possibilities."

"Get an invitation, then come back here."

"But I don't know anybody there yet, how can I get an invitation?"

"If you don't know anybody, go with organised travel."

The businessman became agitated, claiming that he wanted to go to Russia "to help the Russian people." The official shrugged nonplussed and started dealing with the next person in line.

Increasingly Jack and myself began to look down at our own 'invitations', but with much less confidence than we did an hour or so ago. Would that man at the head of the line accept our crucial documents as genuine? He must see hundreds of them every day!

"*Next!* Where do you want to go?" the official asked a thin woman.

"Leningrad," she responded.

"That doesn't exist anymore."

"Uh, well, to the Soviet Union."

"That doesn't exist anymore, either. Can't you be a little clearer?" rebuked the officer.

"I want to visit my mother."

"Where does she live?"

"In Leningrad."

"Really? How does she manage that? Nobody else lives in Leningrad anymore."

The officer was unshaken by the tears slowly filling the woman's eyes.

"She probably means St Petersburg," Laszlo interjected.

"So, you want to go to St Petersburg?" asked the officer of the thin woman. "Why didn't you say so?"

Now it was our turn. We complied and responded as calmly as we could to each of the officer's instructions and questions: "Invitations? Passports? Fifty German Marks each? Got that? Yes? I will call your names when ready."

We took a seat as our documents were passed to somebody in the room behind the window for verification. It was a room stuffed with paperwork and filing cabinets. There was no way our forgery would slip by unnoticed, I thought, smoking one cigarette after another. Even Jack — who doesn't smoke — puffed on a cigarette. The two of us began to resign ourselves to the fact that it was only a matter of time before the police arrived and we were taken away.

"How do you think the Russians will react to our movies?" I asked Jack, in a half-hearted attempt to take our minds off the pressing matter at hand. "Like the crowd last night," he responded, saying nothing more for a while. Then: "Perhaps it would be better to stay in jail over the weekend than to witness such a show again."

The Vörösmozy Marty, the venue for the show of the previous night, a 300-seat downtown theatre, had been a complete sell-out. The show started off well enough, with Jack being greeted by warm applause as he took to the stage to introduce the evening's performance. He spoke (through a translator) about his taste in trash movies —specifically the overblown, typically underfunded movies on exciting subjects that comprised the 'Strange Religious Films' awaiting to be screened.

The nutty Mormon flicks, the Rapture propaganda of the Unarius sect, the urgent warnings of Satan, sex and sin however, failed completely with the Hungarians. Too much talk, and not enough action was the general consensus. Not a good state of affairs for non-subtitled English films playing to a largely non-English speaking crowd. It was the off-kilter narratives and dialogue that turned these particular pictures into bizarre mind-warping masterpieces.

The only thing breaking the silence in the auditorium as the films played, was the giggling of two Americans in the back row. Then came the sound of feet making their way to the exit and doors slamming, as one, two, four Hungarians made their way out — the trickle to the exit soon became a flood. Whole rows started to get up at once — jostling for the exit, and tripping over beer bottles (which rolled noisily down the aisles to the onscreen backdrop of a fire-brand preacher admonishing all and sundry against booze and the wages of sin).

My own memory of that disaster was a little foggy, though, since I had drank quite a bit before the show and had fallen asleep in my seat soon after it started. But the exodus in the dark had awoken me, sort of. My dreams comprised of images of crucifixes, Bibles, virgins, UFOs and a dark and restless Hell from which everybody was suddenly managing to escape.

"Stevenson!... Shengerr!" yelled the officer. The moment had come. Jack and I looked at one another, before silently getting up and making our way over to the window. On the window sill were our passports, the edges of official papers peeking out from between their pages. "Could you please sign here? That's your visa," said the officer. "Have a nice trip."

Phew! These people adhered so closely to their rules that a stamp was a stamp — even a photocopied one.

"Maybe those backwoods Bolshevists never saw a photocopy in their life before," commented Laszlo.

From a stuffy international hotel, I called the Nato Club in Leipzig, Germany, to confirm the rest of our travel arrangements. "Got the visa. You got the flights?"

"Monday morning Leipzig airport, Lufthansa to Moscow," the voice on the other end of the line responded. "Will give them your names in a minute. Everything's okay."

A few days earlier, we had done a show at the Leipzig club, comprising a wildly mixed bag of bizarre Americana: sixties sex educationals, bloody driver instruction films, tornado warnings, advice on rat control, vintage porn, and featurettes preaching against the evils of vandalism and LSD.

A girl goes on an acid trip, bites into a hot dog and the hot dog

screams back at her... A stocky Depression era bum begs for food at the door of an ugly housewife, but gets more than he bargained for when she gives him a bath and forces him to have sex. He happens to be too weak and she kicks him out... A film called *Nothingness* explained to pre-school kids the concepts of, well, 'nothingness'. "It's what a blind man can see," apparently... Also aimed at pre-school children was *The Miracle of Touch*, a film which divulged that "You can touch things that are cold, or hot, or soft, or spiky".

The East Germans in Leipzig didn't speak English any better than the Hungarians, but at least for them the films had a lot more going on visually. Bizarreness, blood and sex — exactly what they expected of American life. The East Germans demanded more and more weirdness, and of course, Jack delivered in spades. Later that night, Torsten, the contented club promoter, took us to a strange meeting where spokespersons for local culture discussed a trip for ten artists to Moscow. Preparations had included two Berlin filmmakers, but since they had failed to get visas, the group was offering Jack and myself the opportunity to be a part of the tour — provided we could arrange to get the visas. Time wise, it would work for us. I had already booked an extensive tour for Jack, but fortuitously the week the Moscow show was planned was still free.

We had two more nights of shows planned in Budapest before heading for Moscow, and — with a change to the programme — these fared somewhat better than the show of the night before. Instead of 'Strange Religious Films' we screened sixties juke box music clips featuring obscure bands like The Standells, who played their music to the accompaniment of bikini-clad chicks swinging their arms, legs and tits. We combined this with crash-test footage, drug scare features, mangled cars and bodies on American highways, porno trailers, and the film *Army Medicine In Vietnam*. America courtesy of its own strange cultural artefacts became an easily palatable, highly enjoyable mondo freak show. That's probably what the Hungarians had expected from the programme in the first place. Now the incomprehensible language was no longer a barrier, it only added to the derangement of the visuals and heightened the weirdness.

Previous page: Red Square.

This page: Zagorsk (top) and a housing project.
Photos: Michael Zettler

Monday morning, Leipzig airport. The troupe of Moscow travellers gathered slowly together, amongst them legendary Cologne underground filmmaker Wilhelm Hein, Leipzig painter Maix, some musicians, journalists, and a couple of Leipzig club promoters. The musicians didn't carry any instruments, the painters no pictures. Wilhelm Hein had a bag of movies however, as did Jack and myself. Now we finally got to hear what the whole trip was about. Executives of the Russian National TV station and the National Filmmakers Association in Russia were responsible for the tour — they had cash and screening spaces on their hands, and so came up with the idea of a 'cultural exchange' programme. No doubt the Russian exchange contingency destined for Germany would comprise a hand-picked selection of artists and the executive organisers themselves — it was, after all, a country they would not otherwise have had the opportunity or resources to visit. A very clever deal, given the fact that the Russians would have their bills paid for by their hosts once in Germany, and had already convinced Lufthansa to sponsor the exchange with free flights for everybody involved.

The flights might have been free but they cost us a lot of waiting around: we had to take a detour via Frankfurt before eventually arriving in Moscow. The halls of Moscow Sheremetyevo airport were dimly lit: wood and dark metal in contrast to the glass and white walls of Western airports. Yet the trappings inside — advertisements for the international duty-free whiskey, perfumes, clocks and cigarettes — were of a distinctly Western flavour. Unlike the old officer in Budapest, here immigration protocol had changed quite a lot since the Soviet days. "Do you want a stamp in

Downtown Moscow.

Previous page:
Old house in Zagorsk (left) and the interior of the fashionable GUM department store on Red Square.
Photos: Michael Zettler

your passport, as a souvenir?" asked the passport inspector. "Only five dollars."

Oleg of the Russian TV station and translator for the group, waited outside in a bus large enough to carry seventy people. "You can use this bus all the time you are here," he announced, "it's yours." Given there were ten of us, that didn't sound quite what we really wanted. On the way into the city, Oleg explained how he expected us to use the bus for tours to the Bolshoi Ballet, the opera, and the Kremlin. Doubtful glances met him. This was such a loose group; with everybody having their own interests and vague personal agendas there was little hope of tourist style excursions taking place. The only people on the trip who had any kind of firm schedule to adhere to were Wilhelm Hein and Jack — they had film shows coming up. Everyone else was simply cattle, here to provide the Russians with an equal number of figures for the exchange programme.

We peered through the windows of the bus for our first impressions of this country. The vista was depressingly bleak: potato fields under grey skies, huge billboards praising Japanese VCRs, and drab concrete settlements in the middle of nowhere.

Our first port of call was a fancy restaurant in Moscow, where we met our Russian exchange partners. Sergei was our main contact during our visit, we learned, a somewhat slippery manager of the Film-maker's Association. He would take care of all the details for the film shows, get our money exchanged on the black market, and was also the one most eager to be on the list of people destined for Germany.

A lavish table had been prepared at the restaurant for the two multicultural groups. Yet there was barely enough champagne to fill the glasses for the official toasts, and so a bottle of Pepsi was given to each guest! Wasn't this supposed to be one of hardest drinking countries in the world? Sergei explained, a little embarrassed, that vodka wasn't served in this establishment, and wine and beer were only sold for Western cash — we would have to order and pay for that ourselves...

Our hosts paid for our meals in roubles, as waiters proudly served cans of German beer for deutschemarks — genuine German supermarket beer cans! It seemed here to be the epitome of fashionable dining.

Over dinner, I discussed with Wilhelm Hein arrangements for the film shows, of which the Russians had set up two. Wilhelm demanded that he take the one at the prestigious House of the Filmmakers; Jack could have the other one, at the university. This sounded okay with me — universities are generally lively places.

The following morning most of the group gathered outside the ten-storey guesthouse of the National Russian TV station, where it had spent the night — just one more high-rise in a neighbourhood of buildings divided by a wasteland of rusty metal, mud and garbage. The bus was already waiting. Today's planned tour was to Zagorsk monastery, regarded as one of Russia's holiest landmarks, Oleg pointed out. Why not give it a shot?

The church had a distinctive multi-layered tower (looking not unlike an onion), and was surrounded by locals peddling decorative Matryoshka dolls — hollow wooden figurines typically painted with the image of a Russian country girl, encasing another similar figurine, encasing another similar figurine... Inside the monastery's gloomy chambers and corridors, sinister-looking monks with long beards swung bowls of incense and read aloud from their Bibles, as women wearing dark scarves prayed with tears in their eyes. The occasional tourist tiptoed by. An uncomfortable place, I quickly convinced Jack that we should get out and explore the seedier side of town.

In the shadow of housing projects, we passed old wooden shacks rotting on muddy side streets. The hand crafted, individualistic shacks had evidently seen better days; now they were stooped as if seeking an escape from the anonymous concrete dwellings that stood nearby. Babushka grandmothers with bent shoulders carried faded shopping bags through the lanes. Although it was only morning, dispirited men in pale-blue work clothes stood outside little stores drinking vodka. Hopelessness and despair everywhere the eye went. It was time to go to church — our type of church.

For such a dump, the town had an amazingly large cinema. A couple of teenagers were there hanging out — no doubt daily customers, acquainted with every corner of its edifice. The movie had already started,

A shop in *Zagorsk*.

a cheap American crime action picture that, to our knowledge, had never played on any American screen outside of showrooms for video merchants. It was dubbed, the Russian way: one male voice reading the main credits, then proceeding to narrate all the dialogue as well. Always the same monotonous tone, unstirred by any of the action taking place, the voice iterated not only the conversations of the male characters, but also of the women, children, indeed anybody talking on screen. Underneath it all the original English soundtrack played faintly. It was as if a rather dull storyteller had taken over the movie, and was presenting it to kids who couldn't be trusted to hear the original version.

Back at the bus Oleg asked, "What did you think? Isn't it great?" — meaning the monastery.

"Yeah, it was cool," I answered. "Just saw a Chuck Norris movie dubbed into Russian at the local movie house."

Oleg looked totally baffled. After that no more group tours with the bus were scheduled.

The next day, preparations got underway for Wilhelm Hein's show at the central palace of Russian filmmaking. The headquarters of the National Filmmaker's Association was a Stalin-era monstrosity of a building near to the Belorussian train station. Outside, the sidewalks had become a hugely busy poverty market where materials stolen from the workplace — light bulbs, plumbing supplies and auto parts — were peddled; old women bartered over worn-out clothes and household items; and peasants praised their home-grown produce... It was a survival sell-out.

By complete contrast, inside the National Filmmaker's Association headquarters, it was deadly quiet, the public excluded from its hallowed halls. Everything was huge — the stairwells, the screening rooms, the non-public restaurant — and everything emanated the air of a faded luxury, unable to shrug the fact that this was once a palace for bureaucrats and censors. The screening room in which Wilhelm's programme was being held had about 200 seats and was bigger than many public cinemas in the West. But... there was no audience. The show had not even been announced to industry insiders. No posters, not even a note. Film producer Sergei had enough clout to organise a film show — and this, apparently, was what he wanted to demonstrate and impress upon his German exchange partners. He was a big whig in a big whig building. Suddenly confronted by our questioning looks at the large empty

Market.
Photos:
Michael Zettler

theatre, it seemed to dawn on Sergei that something crucial was missing for a successful show. Only momentarily embarrassed by the situation, he scratched his head and then set about gathering secretaries from the nearby offices to make up a (meagre) impromptu audience. The show could start — an overview programme of American and German avant-garde films of the last twenty years, comprising of films by Andy Warhol, Bruce Baille, Jonas Mekas, Michael Brynntrup, and some of Wilhelm's own. I had seen all this stuff several times before, but — out of courtesy — stayed so that one more seat might be occupied.

The Russian secretaries weren't quite so tolerant or patient. As soon as the first explicit gay scene appeared on screen, they hurried out of the door. Only Sergei and three or four foreigners remained in the pompous space. After a while, even Sergei left, then Jack and me. Poor Wilhelm was the only one around to witness the end of the show.

Jack's own show was still a couple of days away. We had supplied Sergei with plenty of publicity and background materials for the films that would be playing, so as to avoid us having to make posters in a language we couldn't speak. Yet the Russians couldn't even tell us yet where exactly on the vast university campus our movies would be playing.

We explored the city, a decidedly strange one at that. Rather it was an anti-city that demonstrated how a city *shouldn't* be build. At every turn everything was oversized: streets as wide as oceans of asphalt, flanked by buildings half a mile long — cold, grey, and alienating. The

Red Square was windy and barren, creating an oppressive emptiness that threatened to sink the city into even greater depths of poverty and decay.

We found a wine bar near the Red Square, a dirty basement that sold only one brand of wine at a time. When the supply of that was gone, only then would they switch to another. With each glass came a pickled cucumber. It was self- service. Fat, unfriendly ladies wearing latex aprons worked the table that functioned as a counter. Working class men stumbled through the place, spilling wine over the filthy floor. Two Russians sat themselves at the same table as Jack and myself. One — proudly describing himself as "a waiter in an international hotel" — tried to sell us a watch. I tolerated his diatribe so that Jack could finish his postcard to John Waters, raving to him about how wonderfully trashy it was over here.

Moving on, we found a hole of a bar where the bartender resembled Dolph Lundgren in *Rocky IV*. Hair cropped short, tall and as broad as a wardrobe, he reigned menacingly over his filthy joint with its dirt-crusted tables. I went over to him, noticing the crude tattoos on his bare arms, and a dozen Western beer cans displayed on a shelf behind him. "No beer for sale here," he grunted. "Vodka only."

"What about those cans?" I asked.

"They are empty. Just decoration," he replied. "Get your vodka or get out of here."

Sipping vodka from 100-gram glasses, we watched as the bartender threw a skinny drunk out the door. The drunk came back — it earned him a bloody nose and a kick in the ass, back out the door. The guy's mother, with whom he had been drinking only minutes before being ousted from the place, now got involved. She beat the barman with her

Moscow university.

Previous page: Wilhelm Hein and girlfriend (left), and the black market.
Photos: Michael Zettler

shopping bag, smashing glasses on the counter. The barman simply ducked out of the way. Against a violent mother he was powerless — as a Russian he could never touch her. An intellectual-looking young couple turned to us in embarrassment, excusing their country for the incident taking place and terribly sorry that we — as foreigners — had to witness it. Just then the battling mother hurled a vodka bottle at the glass shelf! What did the Russian intellectuals think entertainment was? We enjoyed it here!

The night of our show had arrived, and Sergei drove us to the university. Upon arriving, he carefully removed the windshield wipers from his car. They would get stolen otherwise, he informed us. The univer-

Jack Stevenson in Moscow.
Photo: Michael Zettler

sity organisers had done a great promotional job — albeit through no fault of their own, a flawed one: around the place hung announcements not only for Jack's show, but for Wilhelm's as well, and also the two Berlin filmmakers who didn't even make it to Moscow. A collage created from European cinema programs, which we had given to Sergei, was pinned to the noticeboard in a totally arbitrary fashion with no indication of which films would be those playing tonight. This information had not made it beyond Sergei. Because of the size and prominence of one particular programme — a programme for a cinema based in Rotterdam — some people showed up for the performance expecting Jack to play 'The Best of the Rotterdam Film Festival'. Most people however had no idea of what to expect — they just assumed it was going to be unusual.

It suddenly became clear that nobody knew the films were going to be in English — another facet of the performance which had failed to make it thus far. The student in charge of the university film club cursed Oleg and Sergei bitterly, sent the German translator away, and headed off to quickly find somebody who could speak English. This he did in a student from India, whose English was particularly smooth and clear. Jack sat with him on stage as he introduced the programme to the crowd of about 300 people, who laughed and cheered riotously throughout. I found this odd as the introduction was a simple one with few discernible jokes. Somebody pointed out to me that the Indian's command of Russian was so poor the audience was actually laughing at him, not Jack's wit.

The impromptu interpreter then had the thankless task of translating the dialogue for each film. A voice-over bereft of a script! Sat in the first row, microphone in hand, he tried valiantly to follow the whacked-out narrations and come up with some approximation in Russian. In an effort to make it all a little more palatable, he'd throw in his own jokes — as he did whenever he got lost. I never got to know whether it was the films or the translation that kept the audience laughing. Whichever, the show was a success, and the crowd was hip enough to appreciate the weird situation.

After the domestic American insanity of sex, death and drugs, we threw in a film especially for our Russian audience. *Red Nightmare* is a 1962 picture warning of the dangers of Communism. It features sixties TV personality Jack Webb, who narrates while perched in front of a sand-bagged machinegun bunker. The story: regular citizen 'Jerry Donovan' takes his liberties a little too much for granted, and is punished by a nightmare: his children cease listening to him, his wife betrays him, and residing in his church is a 'Museum of Communist Inventions'. It's too much. He revolts, only to have his wife and neighbours turn him in to the secret police who swiftly execute him. Time for Jerry Donovan to wake up; time for Jack Webb to reappear and warn the viewer that this is what can be expected of a Communist America. Watch out, and good night.

Red Nightmare was probably the first American Commie-scare film our audience had ever seen, and it left them howling. Only one guy dissented — he missed the joke completely and yelled down from the balcony: "Why are you picking on the Communists?!" The rest of the crowd laughed at him.

After the show, students came over with questions. They asked for the addresses of American horror publications, whether we had seen a particularly obscure Italian zombie movie, where they could obtain Jodorowski tapes, and so on. Their knowledge of Western weirdness was vast and it surprised us.

Wilhelm had been alerted to the announcements around the campus that his programme would also be playing. Loaded with film boxes under each arm, he arrived in time to see that the crowd had left. Moscow hadn't worked out for him... not that the crowd tonight ever looked like they particularly wanted to view art anyway.

Red Nightmare, a movie the trashfilm emissaries screened in Moscow. The daughter volunteers for co-operative farm work, and (main picture) Jerry wakes up.

Next page: Girls with toy guns riding the subway. Photos: Michael Zettler

For most members of the travelling group, Moscow had actually worked out pretty well. A photographer wanting pictures of Moscow street kids and their homes discovered that Russian TV had just made a documentary on the very subject, and they kindly supplied him with a guide. A musician interested in Siberian shaman music was invited by a TV crew on a research trip for a film they were making. As bleak as the city looked and as disorganised many things in it were, there were still plenty of possibilities waiting to be uncovered.

The final night of our visit was celebrated with a party at the dining room of the "House of the Filmmakers", replete with the finest Russian cuisine and enough wine to last through the toasts, the thanks, and the promise of future collaborations. This part of the evening over and the wine depleted, the real night started, with an inexhaustible supply of fast-flowing vodka quickly clouding everyone's mind. Tongues became loose, as horror stories about the Russian Mafia grew wilder and plans for future Moscow projects got bigger. "Splatter fascist!" an envious and disgruntled Wilhelm yelled at me — much to my amusement. He was the only one for whom the trip to Moscow had not worked out particularly well…

Leipzig photographer Misha announced that he knew exactly where to go to witness real Russian underground culture. It was a matter we had bugged Oleg and Sergei about incessantly, but they had no clue as to how they could help. Misha's idea was met with almost universal approval. We grabbed all the vodka we could and out the door we went.

The supply of drink was enough to see us through the subway ride to the other side of town, whereupon Misha led us through side streets and into a dark alley. "There it is!" he exclaimed, pointing to a drab building that showed not the slightest sign of life. Somewhat warily we knocked on the front door, and weren't in the least bit surprised to get

no response. There wasn't any other point of entry we could find, either, but Misha — who by now was so drunk he could hardly stand up — insisted that we were at the right place. "I know it's there," he burbled. "I can see them!"

Finally we accepted that it was all an hopeless vodka-induced delusion, and decided to continue the party back at the guesthouse.

The rest of the night was videotaped for posterity by one of the Leipzig guys. It should have remained in drunken oblivion, where it belonged. Clutching drinks, we all gathered together in a room where Jack had got his hands on a large package of rubber bathing caps. These were the sign of our secret sect, he asserted in a portentous tone, and everybody had to wear one. I refused and Jack eventually gave up on me. "We all are aliens, only here on Earth for a visit," he said with dreamy eyes. "But now we take over the planet... After arriving on Earth in a Rotterdam porno cinema and liking so much what we saw there we have decided to disguise ourselves as human..."

(Jack and I had actually been to an outer-space porn flick in Rotterdam only a few weeks earlier.)

The tape concludes with everybody sprawled out, sleeping in armchairs and on the floor.

It was with aching heads that we arrived at the airport the next morning. We could catch some more sleep on the flight. We passed swiftly through customs — except, what was going on with Jack? I squeezed back down the line to see what happened to him.

He was still dealing with customs.

"No money declaration?" an officer was asking Jack. "You need that. You cannot leave Russia without returning it to customs."

"What's a money declaration?" asked Jack.

"A document you received when you arrived here at the airport," came the reply, and the officer showed Jack a copy of the document.

"I threw it in the garbage this morning," he said. "Didn't know I would need it again. Fuck!"

"Well, you can't leave without the document. It's the law," the officer said. "But if you help me, I may be able to help you."

"What does that mean?" Jack queried.

"I need fifty dollars for a friend and you need to get your plane."

"What about forty? Two twenties?"

"Yes, okay."

The next show on Jack's itinerary was Antwerp, Belgium, then it was across to Holland again. I stayed in Leipzig with a girlfriend. The exciting part of the tour was over. The rest I could supervise by phone.

The Jesus Car

I had been driving all day when finally I left the interstate highway at Detroit's Michigan Avenue exit. According to the map I should have been on the outer fringes of downtown but there wasn't much indication that I'd driven into anything but a debris-strewn wasteland.

At the first red light, a police car pulled alongside me. "Where do you wanna go?" asked the officer, leaning out of the patrol-car window.

"Michigan Avenue, somewhere in the one-thousand numbers," I answered.

"Just take a right and you are there," he said. "Take care. It's not exactly a good neighbourhood."

It certainly didn't look like a good neighbourhood. The few working street lights on Michigan revealed six deserted lanes of broken asphalt, flanked by a long stretch of dilapidated buildings, their windows covered with wooden planks.

I turned into the first gas station I came across — an oasis of neon light, where a few old black men sucked on cans of Budweiser. From here I called the venue that had booked me to screen 'Bi-Coastal Sexperimentals' — the name I had given to a programme of underground short films from New York and San Francisco. I reached Darren, the club owner at his work number. "Just come over," said Darren. "My work place is right behind the club. Look out for an old bank from

Joe Coleman playng 'the Misfit' in *Black Hearts Run Red*, in front of the Jesus Car. *Photo: Jeri Rossi* the 1920s. Never mind that it's all barred up. Drive into the courtyard behind it and I will meet you there."

The derelict bank was easy enough to spot. The courtyard behind it was a wrecked parking lot for huge and heavily dented seventies cars. Cars like the one I was driving. At the end of the lot I noticed a small building with a light, outside of which somebody was waving his arms and yelling: "Johannes? Is that you?" It was Darren.

"I've got a really cool job here," Darren explained. "I'm the security man for the auto parts factory you see back here — one of the few auto-related factories left in town. And it also happens to be the backlot of my own club, which is in that building you see over there. So I basically get paid to watch my own building at night.

"You won't believe how many scavengers there are here at night, breaking into buildings whether they think they're abandoned or not. They break off everything and steal whatever they can get their hands on. Tim, the guy who put you in contact with me, is one of the worst of them, actually. You should see what he got out of film labs…"

Detroit was a Pompeii of the industrial age, according to Darren. Except that it didn't take a volcanic eruption to bury the place — a few economic ones in the seventies were enough. The auto industry, on which the city thrived, left town and with it four of its five million inhabitants. They found a future — or maybe not — someplace else.

The result was that whole neighbourhoods were left abandoned. On a more positive note, the place was cheap. "I could never afford a building like this in any other American city," confided Darren. "But of course, I have to bar it up like the other buildings, otherwise I would be robbed every night. And besides, I sell liquor without a license, so I have to maintain a low profile…"

The late shift at the auto parts factory was at an end. Black men wearing faded blue denims clocked off and dispersed through the car park, nosily starting their worn-out Sedans and heading off into the night.

"Is there any place to eat around here?" I asked. "Well, there are two kinds of burger places," Darren advised. "The kind where rat tails stick out of the burgers, and the other kind where they chop them off." After pondering for a long moment on which car would draw less attention — my battered old made-in-Detroit one, with the New York license plates, or his eighties Nissan with the Michigan plates — we headed

Michigan Avenue in Detroit.

Previous page: The bank in Detroit (building on the right).
Photos: Allan Barnes

off to some late-night white-trash hang-out, where the juke box played early Joe Cocker and tattooed bikers cruised for a fight.

"What kind of crowd are you expecting for tomorrow night's show?" I asked Darren. He was a little hesitant: "You see, since I live on the liquor sales in that place, I can't really do that much advertising. We tend to work through word of mouth, but should get a cool crowd."

He didn't sound very convincing.

After spending the night on a camping bed in the cold hall of the dusty bank, I was awoken by Tim, the famous scavenger. "Hi. Glad to meet you. I guess we have some work to do today."

Tim told me that the equipment Darren had in the place was all trash, and there was no way I should do a show with it. Darren had no Super-8 equipment at all, and his impressive vintage 16mm projectors had ceased to pick up sound tracks.

And so it was I drove with Tim downtown.

What a downtown! Skyscrapers — they had plenty of them in Detroit. "They're all empty," said Tim. "Fifty floors of dust and roaches."

Playboy Voodoo

With the exception of a few bums inspecting the trash outside fast food joints, very few people were on the streets. We pulled up outside a club where Tim thought we might be able to borrow a working projector. Next to the door was a guy banging his head against the wall. "Hey, how you doing?" asked Tim. The guy just went on banging his head. "He's an old friend of mine," Tim explained. "But he's not always in a talkative mood."

There was no projector to be had here or at any of the other clubs that we went to; nobody seemed willing to lend Tim any equipment of any kind. Some of the people we asked said whatever they gave to Tim would come back broken, while others said they wouldn't get anything they gave to Tim back at all. When all looked hopeless, Tim remembered some "good friends". Unfortunately, the highway exit which would lead us to these "good friends" was closed. We took the next one. Tim didn't know the address or the name of the precise area in which these good friends of his lived anyway, and so we ended up just driving around some fucked-up neighbourhood, unable to even ask for directions. I took the car down one street after the next, hoping Tim would eventually recognise something.

Eventually he did, and we came away with a couple of projectors. They were working, but their condition was questionable to say the least.

During my tour with Tim through Detroit's supposedly "cool" clubs, I saw only one of my posters — this in spite of the fact that I had printed up a few hundred and mailed them off to him weeks ago. There was nothing in the local press either. At about 7pm, Tim and I arrived back at the "Bank".

Word of mouth brought about fifteen people to the show. Fifteen people who sat waiting with their cans of beer as Tim and I tried to get the equipment to work. We discovered that the projectors were missing parts, whilst the bulb in one blew on its test run. It came as no surprise to me that we didn't have a replacement.

Suddenly a girl walked in, a projector in her hands. "You called me this morning..." she said. Indeed, we had. Given the sheer volume of equipment we had accumulated by this point, we were able to come up with something vaguely workable. It meant that Tim had to spend the entire show holding a microphone and feeding sound from the construct-projector's built-in speaker to the venue's 'sound system' — such as it was.

Amazingly enough, after all our initial troubles, no technical fuck-ups hindered the performance. Amongst the films that played were Richard Kern's *Fingered* and *Manhattan Love Suicides*, Greta Snider's punk-warehouse-community home-porn *Shred of Sex*, Tessa Hughes-Freeland/Ela Troyano's erotic collage *Playboy Voodoo*, and Jeri Rossi's *Black Hearts Bleed Red*.

In the latter film, a constantly quarrelling family goes on a trip only to get stopped by felons on a dirt track and executed. The leader of the killer gang, a character named The Misfit, is played by painter/performance artist Joe Coleman, who arrives at the scene in a battered grey 1973 Dodge Dart, the face of Jesus painted on each headlight.

It was in this very same car that I had travelled to Detroit from New York, and which was now parked outside. It was in this car that I would head out west in the morning... with the movie that featured it loaded in the trunk.

II

A few months before the show in Detroit, in Spring 1993, I had arranged for San Franciscan trash movie collector Jack Stevenson to come
to the Millennium Film Workshop in New York and exhibit his programme of exploitation movie trailers and outtakes. I was half joking
when, after the show, I asked him if he knew of any summer jobs on the
West Coast — New York City being too hot and humid for me at that
time of the year. "You know Dennis Nyback in Seattle, don't you?" he
replied. "He's looking for somebody to run his cinema for a time during
summer. He needs to leave town but doesn't want the place closed
while he's gone."

I called Dennis the very next day.

"You know how to run a cinema?" Dennis asked me. "You've done that
kind of thing before, in Germany, right?"

"Sure," I said, and we quickly made a deal: I would pay Dennis $25
overhead per day, and the cinema would be mine for a few weeks. I
could show whatever I wanted, keep any profit I made and stay in his
apartment for free.

It didn't take me long to come up with a programme that I considered an all-out attack on the taste and nerves of my prospective audience, with films ranging from Amos Poe's *Subway Riders*, featuring John Lurie as saxophone-playing serial killer, a variety of Cinema of Transgression underground shorts, Jim Van Bebber's violent gang action picture *Deadbeat at Dawn*, Danish animal porn, through to a weekend-long Kuchar festival. Movies that were "strange... bizarre... violent... pornographic... ART & SLEAZE & FUN", as I was later to announce to the Seattle press.

While I was calling up filmmakers and programming movies for the cinema, Jeri Rossi happened to tell me she was moving out of her Williamsburg apartment and into Manhattan, which meant that she would have to let her car with the Jesus headlights go. "A car in Manhattan is just too much of a headache," she said. "I won't need it there, anyway."

Jim VanBebber (left) and Ric Walker in *Deadbeat at Dawn*.
Photo courtesy: Jim VanBebber

I asked her how much she wanted for it. "Maybe $200," she said.

A plan was hatching in my head. "Do you think the car could make it over to the West Coast?" I asked.

"It needs a few things fixing," replied Jeri. "But basically I think it should make it."

I decided there and then that I would buy the car and drive it across America, with movies in the trunk.

The car had history, belonging to a variety of underground artists before Jeri acquired it. It had belonged to performance artist Karen Finley. She sold it to Joe Coleman, who painted Jesus on the headlights and in turn handed it over to Jeri Rossi.

In a few days, it would be mine.

The car was big and grey, made from metal thick enough to give one the impression of riding in a tank. It had plenty of knocks and dents in it, too, having survived quite a few hairy incidents on the road.

The repairs that Jeri had said were needed didn't sound too big a problem. *The engine had to run idle for ten minutes before the car would move?* I wasn't in a hurry. *The speedometer bore no relation to the actual speed the car was travelling, jumping constantly back and forth between zero and 120mph?* Who needs a speedometer anyway? *The safety belts were useless?* I felt safe enough. *The radio didn't work?* I could carry a cassette player on the passenger seat. *The brakes were worn out?* Maybe I should have somebody look into that particular point...

In the middle of July 1993, I headed out of New York for Seattle, doing the one-night show in Detroit on the way...

III

The rain was heavy as I drove down the Cascades toward Puget Sound and into Seattle. The Dodge was in better shape than I could have hoped, and got through the entire journey without a hitch. Not withstanding the emission of thick blue exhaust fumes whenever I engaged the car in its early morning warm-up — I annoyed more motel residents than I can remember, and panicked passers-by in Madison, Wisconsin, who believed I was attempting suicide in the basement car park of the hotel.

Aside from that, the trip along the interstate had been without incident. My cassette player provided the empty highway with a sound-track of Hong Kong pop, rolling by under a scorching sun the dairy farms of Wisconsin and Minnesota, the brown plains of North Dakota and Eastern Montana, hitting the foggy Rockies of Idaho and through the rainy desert in the Eastern part of Washington State.

Looking for Dennis Nyback's Pike Street Cinema, I cruised the deserted Capitol Hill section of Pike Street, which was isolated from downtown by a huge bridge. "It's in the worst block of the street," Dennis had informed me, but that wasn't much help — it was a street of vintage brick buildings, none of which looked anything close to being well-maintained. No bright cinema lights anywhere. Neither was Dennis picking up his phone.

Quite some time passed before eventually I found the place — a dark storefront window over which a poster for *Hunter Mann's Highway Cinema* was taped, and above it, in hand-painted letters, 'Pike Street Cinema.' The place was closed — no wonder I had so much trouble finding it.

It was bad news if I couldn't reach Dennis — I would have to spend my last forty bucks on a motel room.

Up the street was a crowded hipster bar called the Comet Tavern, where I decided to hang out for a while over some beers and see if I couldn't get hold of Dennis later. Not a wise decision as it turned out. I didn't get hold of Dennis, but spent enough of my cash that I had no choice but to drive around town for half the night looking for a place cheap enough that I could now afford to stay. Come the bright and sunny morning I was flat broke. But I did find Dennis at the cinema. Blonde, clean shaved and dressed in a suit of an indefinable vintage era, he looked like a Wall Street broker from around the first half of the century. Humming jazz tunes from the thirties, he was busy rewinding the films of Hunter Mann, while Hunter himself was down in the lobby repairing a bicycle. Mann, with his ponytail and worn-out T-shirt, looked the polar opposite of Nyback, and every inch a natural part of poverty row cinema.

Dennis seemed to be an alien element even in his own surroundings. The theatre was an ill-lit, narrow space containing about sixty-five dirt-

The author outside the Pike Street Cinema in Seattle.

stained seats, the walls were covered with tatty old theatre curtains, and the small projection loft resembled a cross between a garbage dump and a film collector's attic. Here were crammed hundreds of rusty metal film cans, mouldy cardboard boxes and cartons filled to the hilt with unspecified 35mm movie trailers — every square inch of which was covered in dust.

"You made it!" Dennis greeted me. "I didn't really believe you would, after what people in New York told me about your car."

"The car's fine," I said. "It's right out front. In a way, it's like a rolling version of your cinema — old and battered but still going regardless."

I asked Dennis about the strange sounding programme he had been playing the last couple of days.

"Oh, that was Hunter Mann's bicycle cinema. A pretty strange operation. The guy travels through the hinterlands of the US by bicycle, showing films. He's down in the lobby right now..."

I took my old typewriter out of the car and set to work on texts and exploitative headlines for my programme, while at the same time I chatted with Hunter Mann.

"Every summer I get a programme of experimental films together," Mann told me, "then go to some backwoods area of the United States and bicycle around. I visit all these small towns where there was never any cinema, or there was but it closed down back in the fifties, or whatever. I talk the local hotel into letting me stay for free, convince some farmer into letting me use his barn, or the mayor into letting me use the town hall, or whatever space is available. Then I distribute flyers and let everybody in town know I'm putting on a show, which I do on my own screen and with my own 16mm projector — it's all here in my bicycle trailer."

I was curious. "How does it work financially?"

"The shows are for free. People give me food or invite me to dinner, and sometimes they let me stay at their place. I never charge anything. I actually work all year long to finance these trips. I just want people to see real movies projected onto real screens. Most people in these small towns know nothing other than TV — a lot of them have never seen a movie projected onto a screen before."

"How do they react to the films being experimental? I mean, it must be highly unusual for them?"

"Oh, they love it," said Mann. "They don't really care what's on the screen; the projected image alone is something great to them."

Mann told me that he was from the Seattle area, and had just started his latest summer tour at Dennis' Pike Street Cinema. "It went alright. Not too big a crowd. I'm better in the countryside where there's no competition..."

I couldn't imagine Mann had much competition over the whole of the US. Soon enough, he had his bike and trailer ready and was pedaling out of town.

My flyers were finished. Well, almost. I just needed a little lay-out equipment, a copy shop and about twenty bucks to print a few hundred of them. I asked Dennis if he could lend me the cash to run off the flyers and to see me through another day, at least until my programme started and I could pay him back. But smartly attired Dennis was flat broke himself.

"I hardly have enough dough for gas to get me out of town," he said. "But why don't you take this jar of coins? It should get you going." And he handed me an old preserve jar, filled with quarters and dimes.

My kind of advertising made Dennis nervous. He studied the big window display I had created, and said, "I don't want to censor you, but putting up photos of penises in the window might bring the Vice Squad."

Little pictures of dicks with eyeglasses painted on them were part of my advertising for Pam Kray's *Penis Puppets*, a short film featuring talking male genitalia, animated by thin thread from behind a puppet stage.

"What would they do if they showed up?" I asked. "Fine me?"

"They might put you in jail," said Dennis. "I spent a day in jail when I was working as a projectionist and came up with advertising like that for the Green Parrot porno theatre."

"A day in jail sounds cool to me," I told him. "The best way to get into the papers and my programme known."

"My cinema paid for a lawyer who got me out of there," Dennis retorted. "Nobody is going to pay a lawyer for you here..."

I didn't take the little dicks out of my advertising campaign — and the Vice Squad didn't care.

Pam Kray who made the *Penis Puppets* movie, as well as *Piss Mission* and *Consenting Children* — which displayed a similarly humorous bent — was actually my assistant for the Seattle stint. Travelling from San Francisco, she arrived at Seatac airport that very afternoon. I had enough gas in my car to pick her up and she had enough cash to see me through to our first show.

Dennis left town on his tour of the mid-west, ready to screen vintage movies from his collection and catch a few baseball games in Cleveland and Chicago. The "Bank" in Detroit had booked him for a whole week and he wasn't particularly looking forward to it, after hearing my account of how the place was run.

My first weekend of shows at the Pike featured a programme of New York Underground shorts, vintage American sex educational films — "campy school day shorts about dating, venereal disease, child birth, dangerous perverts and divorce" as I described them in my programme notes — and Pam Kray's Super-8 atrocities.

There was no air-conditioning, I discovered when on my first weekend at the Pike Street Cinema we were struck by a heat wave. Only a handful of people made it into the sweat box that the cinema had suddenly become.

The press tended to greet my programme with some apprehension. Take for instance the comment of a reporter for the *Seattle Weekly*:

PIKE STREET CINEMA

Curator Dennis Nyback is on vacation, but the weirdness takes no hiatus. Guest curator Johannes Schonherr, a long-time curator of cult cinema shows in Germany, takes over the reins. Through August 8, he's presenting underground, cult, banned, buried, and otherwise not generally available (nor sometimes desirable) films. Topics range from the campy — fifties sex education with titles like VD Epidemic — to the disgusting (a Danish film about an "animal porn queen")...

Yet, the word was out, thanks in part to papers like *The Stranger* and the *Urban Spelunker*, where it was announced I intended to play *Hated* — Todd Phillips' brand new but already notorious documentary on punk rocker GG Allin who, after a final violent gig at the Gas Station in New York, had died just a few weeks earlier.

This was to be the first screening of *Hated* outside of New York City, and for the whole weekend the phone was ringing almost off the hook.

"When's the GG movie on?" I was asked over and over again...

Pike Street Cinema programme.

Next page:
The Murder Junkies.
Photo: Todd Phillips

IV

Only a few days before his death, I had been introduced to GG Allin by Richard Kern during a rare screening of Kern's early *Zombie Hunger* at New York's CBGB. In the movie a guy shoots heroin and then goes on to demolish the apartment the film was shot in, sparing only the filmmaker and his camera in his destructive drive. "It was my apartment and he really smashed it," Kern told me after the film. "In those days I didn't give a shit."

GG himself wasn't in any kind of destructive mood that night. We went over to CB's Gallery, drank beer, talked about his plans for a European tour, and his hopes that I would screen Todd Phillips' documentary in as many places in Europe as possible. (This I did some time later.)

A complete contrast however, was the GG I saw in action on June 27 at the Gas Station on Avenue B and 2nd Street. It had been a slow afternoon at the club, with boring poser bands playing in the little hall tucked behind a jungle of rusty metal sculptures. The place was the private nuthouse of a welding lunatic. Up to fifteen feet in height, these sculptures — these piles of trashed metal — were interconnected with heavy steel beams. A car rested on one of them, nestled way up over the heads of the assembled beer swilling punk rockers. Mothers in torn fishnet stockings lay in the sun, yelling after their blue-haired children. Hardly anybody bothered to walk inside and listen to Humyn Sewage, Denied or whatever other band was on the bill. Suddenly, a very agitated GG broke through the metal gate, wearing nothing but a leather jacket, a G-string and heavy boots. He was escorted by his brother Merle and the rest of his band, the Murder Junkies — Dino, the drummer, and bearded Bruce Weber.

"GG! GG!" yelled the crowd. The Murder Junkies took to the stage and within minutes, had their instruments plugged in and were starting to rock. For the first number, GG removed his jacket and G-string, squatted and shat on the stage. Pure GG — as I knew him from the movie and the many stories I had heard; the 'anti-social animal' that wanted to put danger back into Rock'n'Roll.

The ritual continued with GG smearing the shit over himself and hurling handfuls of it into the audience. A girl in the first row moved close to take some photos, holding the camera right up to GG's face. He tore her glasses off, trampled them, then squeezed the girl's face between his thighs, all the while singing into his mic. Media conscious as he was, he left the camera intact, which disappeared into the heaving crowd with the girl the moment she was free.

Nobody wanted to get in GG's way but neither did they want to miss seeing anything violent when it did happen — and it did happen, continuously. "Stop dancing!" GG yelled at one bunch of youngsters, driving home his point by beating their noses bloody. The band wasn't able to complete the third number, because the Gas Station manager pulled the plug on the sound. It had been relatively easy to avoid GG's fists up to now, but liberated from the microphone cord he proceeded to punch his way through the whole little venue, with the screaming audience as his soundtrack. He rammed his bald head through a glass window — and suddenly he was out in the yard, wielding a steel bar and ready to kill. Mercilessly he bashed everybody crossing his path, chasing bloody faced punks with bad haircuts around the steel art. A thousand times GG had claimed that one day he would commit suicide on stage and take with him as many people in the audience as he could. *Was this the day?* Everyone who attended the show knew exactly what it was they were getting into (with the possible exception of the stupid mothers who had brought along their kids). As tended to be the case with all his shows, GG whipped up the crowd until they exploded with violence and fought back. It was a few hundred people against one, and GG retreated. Suddenly, he was over on the other side of Avenue B, naked, shit-smeared and bleeding from wounds all over his body. Many of the people who had moments ago been running away from him, suddenly became 'courageous' and from a distance started to throw beer bottles at GG.

Police cars with their sirens howling arrived on the scene. A few bottles were thrown in their direction also, but — no doubt quite deliberately — fell wide of the mark. It seemed nobody wanted to get into a *real* fight and have the riot squad move in. GG seized the opportunity to make his escape, but wasn't able to get far. While the confused police remained outside the Gas Station, a parade of about a hundred people followed GG down the street. He wanted nothing more than to lose the throng chasing him and

GG Allin live at the Gas Station,
New York City — his final gig.
Photos: Todd Phillips

chanting "GG! GG!" But, like some bleeding martyr, he was the reluctant spearhead of a procession that had vivid hair colours, which emptied trash cans onto the sidewalks and smashed the windows of parked cars. GG made it to Avenue A and Houston and climbed into a taxi cab, only to have the terrified driver dart out and flag down a passing police car. The cops didn't know what was happening, and resorted to pulling GG from the cab whilst attempting to disperse the crowd. To no avail. GG ran off down Essex Street, then onto Stanton — Puerto Rican territory. Men playing dominoes and women smoking crack out on their porches had never seen anything like it. They followed the parade with their mouths open wide. Somebody managed to get some clothes to GG, and partially dressed he had more success with a cab after getting back on Houston. It was the last I saw of him...

The next morning Jeri Rossi called me and told me that GG Allin was dead.

"That can't be true," was my response. "I saw him only last night at his show."

"He died last night," she elaborated. "His brother just called me. He OD'd after the show."

I called Richard Kern to see if he could corroborate the story.

"Have you already heard the news?" he said down the line before I was able to ask. "GG is dead."

I wouldn't speak to many people who hadn't already heard the news.

Later that day, I rang Todd Phillips with a proposition: "This may sound like exploitation at its most base, but I have *Hated* booked for just two days in Seattle — I want to extend that."

Todd started to laugh. "GG would have liked *that*! Book it for as many days as you want!"

There were only a few days remaining before Todd was set to embark on a run of *Hated* himself. As good a film as it was, it seemed no theatre in New York had wanted to play a documentary on as vile a character as GG Allin. Todd simply rented a cinema in order to screen it — Jonas Mekas' avant-garde bastion, the Anthology Film Archives, of all places.

With GG's death of course, the situation quickly changed. It was for a short time hip to talk about GG Allin, and related articles appeared in the press. He even made it onto the front page of the *New York Post* and into the Obituary section of the *New York Times*.

V

If I had shown only *Hated* and nothing else during my tenure at the Pike Street, I would have left town a rich man. People queued down the block for that film, and many came back to see it a second time. With eighty-five

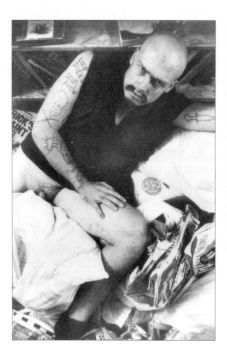 

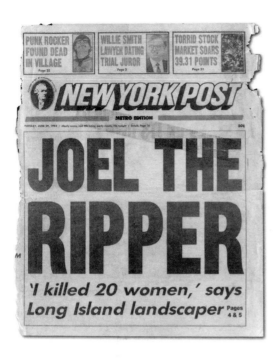

Posthumously, GG makes the front page of the *New York Post*.

Previous page: Photo shoot on GG Allin's last day alive.
Photos: Richard Kern

people the theatre was filled to capacity. Any more than this and the audience spilled into the aisles, while some people even climbed up to the beams protruding from the make-shift projection booth and balanced there. They just wanted in, whether they were able to see the screen or not.

The same nights as I ran *Hated*, I would have another movie playing. This was clearly announced as a different show to *Hated* and for which I charged admission separate from the *Hated* show — yet people still bought tickets for this expecting to see *Hated*. The Pike Street screened the GG Allin movie — that was all these people knew and cared about. Many left the theatre aghast. GG shitting on screen and smashing in faces was one thing, they had come expecting to see that, but… *Animal Lover*?

A forty-minute Danish 'documentary' from the early seventies, *Animal Lover* is about farm girl/porn star Bodil Jensen who liked to have sex with animals: her dog, her pig, her horse. Famous porn producer Alex DeRenzy had picked up the film of Bodil and added another thirty minutes of 'introduction'. This comprised of the sleaziest narrator in the history of American cinema talking about the act of sodomy and conducting a — no doubt fake — interview with a girl who claimed to have been kidnapped while hitchhiking through Morocco. She relates the story of how she was raped by a bunch of Moroccans who then let their dog have her when they got tired of her themselves. The actual gross-out however came with the second reel — the "documentary you are about to see" part of the show that the narrator never tired of heralding — which depicted in detail Bodil screwing her animal friends.

GG Allin's funeral. Dino, the Murder Junkies' drummer, stands on the left.
Photos: Todd Phillips

VI

Over the weekend, the GG craze had to take a backseat. I had a Kuchar festival booked, with guest appearances by Mike and George Kuchar, and actress Marion Eaton. Initially my plan was to drive down to San Francisco, pick them up and bring them over to Seattle. A thirty-hour round trip. George resisted the idea with a vengeance and convinced me it would be better to shell out the dough for plane tickets — if I wanted them to attend the show, that was.

As it turned out, the plane was the better option. I was used to the idiosyncrasies of the car; George wasn't. He arrived in Seattle a day ahead of his brother and Marion, and eyed the Dodge with which I had come to collect him with deep suspicion. "With *this* we go to the city?" he exclaimed.

The car punished George by turning the short trip to town into a nightmare for him. He fought fiercely with his mangled seat belt all the way, while the ventilation system blew a pungent gasoline smell into his face, compelling him to stick his head out of the window and into the rain.

"Great car, isn't it?" I said.

I asked George if he minded whether I smoked.

"Go ahead," he replied. "But I will have to puke."

George noticed the steam arising off the hood of the car. "What's that? Is the car going to catch fire?"

"It's just the rain vaporising," I guessed, not quite sure myself.

George was ecstatic that we had made it to Dennis' apartment in one piece. He never set foot in the Jesus car again.

Things got worse the next day. It was a sunny morning and I was quite happy as I sped towards the airport to pick up Marion and Mike.

The temperature gauge, I noticed, was rising and quickly passed the red danger mark. The arrow didn't stop its ascension until it hit the top and physically could not move any further. I took the next exit and pulled over. Expecting the worst, I slowly lifted open the hood. From the engine — invisible under a dense cloud of steam — came the agitated sound of boiling water. Shit! There was little else I could do but start the car up again and take it down to a restaurant parking lot conveniently situated not too faraway. I almost killed two bikers as I took the shortest route up a one-way street, impressive bursts of steam rising from beneath the engine hood. I ran into the restaurant — more a bar — and breathlessly barked questions at the waitress: "What's the number of the local cab company? Where are we? What's the name of this place?"

With the arrival of the cab, I made it to the airport just in time to catch Mike and Marion stepping out of the gate. Marion laughed heartily when she heard what had happened. She expressed relief that she hadn't had to drive all the way from San Francisco with George, who more likely would have spent the whole time filming the adventure.

We took a mini van bus back into town.

The festival could start — one of the most complete Kuchar festivals ever, as it turned out. Mike had brought along his old 8mm projector, and I had managed to borrow a reel-to-reel tape recorder, enabling us to show the brothers' rarely screened early masterpieces, such as *Night of the Bomb* (whose notoriety is that George stood in for an actress too embarrassed to get undressed for a rear-nudity scene). It also meant that we could show the incredibly wild and colourful *Lust for Ecstasy*, and *Lovers for Eternity*, the latter bringing Kuchar star Donna Kerness and New York underground luminary Jack Smith together on one screen. George's classic *Hold Me While I'm Naked* was on the agenda, so too Mike's *Sins of the Fleshapoids*, the film that supposedly had a career-making impression on the young John Waters. The midnight shows were reserved for the most whacked out of all the Kuchar works — George Kuchar and Curt McDowell's *Thundercrack!* Adhering to the creaky convention of an old black-and-white haunted house movie, *Thundercrack!* rubs explicit sex into the mix.

As a violent thunderstorm rages, several groups of strangers are forced to seek refuge in a remote mansion, inhabited by an alcoholic Marion Eaton. The place begins to slowly divulge its terrible secrets as the guests become increasingly entangled in both straight and gay sexual relationships...

Mike, George and Marion gave magnificent introductions to the movies, answered many and varied questions from the audience, and ensured me they had a thoroughly good time. Well, I was glad to hear it — considering we only averaged seven people per show. The phone hadn't stopped ringing the entire festival with the same old question being asked of me each time I picked it up: what time did the GG Allin movie start?

Seattle was not a movie town. Everybody was into punk and grunge rock, happy to stick with the clubs at night. They didn't care about movies that didn't feature famous underground rock stars.

At night, the Kuchars and Marion crammed into Dennis' small apartment. Pam had evacuated to friends living locally, while I retreated to a sofa in the cinema, its auditorium bathed in a twilight glow whenever I left the curtains open. "I could never sleep there," Dennis told me later. "It's eerie at night." It was, but I liked sitting there with a six-pack of beer, dozing off whilst listening to the garbled voices and music that drifted through the thin wall from the white trash bar next door. The Eagles' Hotel California came up on the jukebox almost every second song. Lord knows why those guys next door liked that song so much. Most of them lived in the flop-house-type pads above the cinema and down the block, "where you can check out any time you like but you can never leave" — as the Eagles would put it.

I had been to the bar next door once with Pam and a few locals. We ordered a pitcher of Red Hook beer. Red Hook is supposed to be red, but what we got wasn't. "This ain't Red Hook," we complained. "It sure is," was the response from the stone-faced old Japanese bartender. "You ordered Red Hook, you got Red Hook."

Some of the regulars shouted over: "Hey man, we saw you. You mixed the Red Hook with Mount Ranier, the cheap beer!"

Without saying a word, the bartender emptied our pitcher into the sink and filled it afresh — this time with the stuff we were paying for. "Welcome to Hotel California..." sang the Eagles on the jukebox.

At the back of the cinema was a dark, narrow alley, lined with garbage cans. A few months before I arrived, a fight between two guys in the apartment upstairs spilled out into the yard, resulting in one of the guys being stabbed to death on our back doorstep. Mia Zapata, singer in a punk band called The Gits and a good friend of Pam, was last seen on the street around the corner one night, only to be discovered the next day strangled in the woods. After that, Pam was always a little hesitant about walking down Pike Street alone at night. Somebody else was bludgeoned to death in one of the upstairs apartments, but nobody seemed to know much about that particular case. One night, when I was closing up the theatre, a squadron of siren wailing, light-flashing cop cars and ambulances pulled up and stormed the building next to the cinema. They re-emerged with a blood-spattered guy in handcuffs and a woman on a stretcher. "He attacked her with a hatchet," neighbours said. I queried one of the cops. "Just some domestic violence," he replied, playing down the incident.

A lot of Seattle-ites did consider the block to be dangerous, which didn't help to fill the cinema. I liked the area however, and my favourite bar, the Comet Tavern, was just up the street. It was a place in which a lot of my audience hung out, and where I could go to hang flyers whilst sipping beer. It suddenly stopped being cool at around 1.30 at night, however, when the bartenders rigidly enforced the 2am State closing law. "Gulp down your beer or we'll take it away," they demanded whilst making a grab for the glass in your hand. At 1.45 they had the place cleared out... which left just enough time to pick up a six-pack at the gas station, before they too closed the sale of beer.

As the Kuchars were busy giving one interview over breakfast, and avoiding another one over lunch — for which a guy from a local gay

Eclipse of the Sun Virgin

magazine had showed up wearing a skirt — I tried to remember where I'd left the damn car. It was in a car park outside a restaurant, but I had no idea of the name of the area or the exit I'd taken to get it there. There was only one solution, and I set off on foot down the side streets that ran parallel to the highway. It took me three hours of walking under the glaring sun, through industrial estates and truck parking lots, before finally I found the place. The fifty dollars I had invested for a membership in the AAA auto club started to pay off: I got the car towed for free.

I don't know too much about the workings of the motor vehicle, but I could understand that the big hole in the engine block to which the mechanic was pointing wasn't a good thing. His explanation for the breakdown was long, having something to do with the freeze plug falling out. Two days after repairing the thing, the car broke down again — this time in Capitol Hill. The same mechanic put it right, swearing to God that this new freeze plug would hold for all eternity.

The Kuchars and Marion took the mini van to the airport for their return flight.

Donna Kerness (left), plus Albert Salzano and friend in the Kuchar brothers' *Lust for Ecstacy*.

VII

The new week started with another run of *Hated*. The second feature was Amos Poe's *Blank Generation*, a 1975 out-of-sync punk documentary filmed in and around New York clubs like CBGB and Max's Kansas City. I had booked it in the hope that footage of Patti Smith, Television, Wayne County, and the Ramones would draw in the people of Seattle. Draw them it did, lots of them, most of whom wanted to see the Ramones.

Blank Generation began to play. At the point when the Ramones were supposed to appear on screen a piece of white leader ran through the projector — but no Ramones. The frantic search for an explanation led me to a small piece of yellow paper in the film box. On it was a note in Swedish: 'Ramones removed' was all I could decipher. With the rest of the film still playing behind me, I called Amos Poe in New York. He was shocked. It was his only print and he had no idea that the Ramones were missing. I made a short apologetic speech to the angry crowd in the theatre, and gave them *Fingered* as a bonus. It proved to be punk enough a substitute for the five minutes of Ramones they had missed, and they went away afterwards relatively satisfied.

For its subsequent performances over the next few days, I told every customer who showed up to buy a ticket for *Blank Generation* that the Ramones footage had been stolen.

Also on the bill for my final weekend at Pike Street were the films of Richard Kern. "Richard who?" was the question invariably asked of me whenever anyone called inquiring about upcoming shows. Those Seattle-ites know nothing but their friggin' music!

"Kern played in a band with GG Allin," I would explain. "He also made movies with Foetus, Henry Rollins and Lydia Lunch." This the callers were able to grasp.

Neither did the name John Lurie ring a bell. "See John Lurie as saxophone-playing serial killer," was how I announced the screening of Amos Poe's *Subway Riders*. Lurie was a musician, but his New York post-punk jazz didn't go down awfully well in Seattle — the few adventurous souls who did make it to the screenings quickly left in bewilderment.

To complicate things further, *Subway Riders* does indeed feature Lurie as a saxophone-playing killer, but not all the way through. Suddenly, without warning, the role played by Lurie is taken over by someone who looks nothing like him, and who evidently can't play the saxophone hanging around his neck. The substitute Lurie is director Poe himself, forced to step in after Lurie simply walked off the set, never to return.

Poe had told me the story behind the incident: Johanna Heer, the cinematographer, had promised there was a substantial grant from her native Austria on its way to help finance the film. According to Poe, everybody on the set hated Heer ("She is the worst person in the world," was how Poe described her), and when it became clear that the grant money was just a mirage, Lurie quit. Not that it prevented *Subway Riders* from becoming one of the most successful cult movies of the early eighties, with crowds in New York and Europe going nuts over it. Maybe the mind-set of the Seattle population was structured differently...

It was Johanna Heer to whom I had to turn in order to rent the film. I talked to her on the phone a couple of times and — as much as I liked what she did on *Subway Riders* — it was never a pleasure. My impression was that she considered her camerawork on the film more important than Poe's direction. Heer wanted a substantial sum of money for the loan of the print, and the promise that I would include her name in my programme schedule. I first had to fax the schedule over to her in Vienna as proof that I was complying with the agreement, before she would let the film go. I'm not usually in the habit of including the names of camera people in my schedule...

The third movie that weekend was Jim Van Bebber's *Deadbeat at Dawn*, which I had announced as a "punk-gang-splatter-action from Dayton, Ohio", thinking it to be the kind of language the local grungeheads might understand. Some of them did.

VIII

Dennis returned from the Mid-West. He was broke and disgusted at how badly organised his Detroit shows were, but happy to see his cinema still standing. For Pam and me, it was time to hit the road again — down to San Francisco, where Pam had arranged a three-hour programme combining underground shorts I had brought from the East Coast and the San

Franciscan premiere of *Hated*. Jack Stevenson forwarded to me advance press on the show and it sounded as if the whole town was waiting for us.

On Monday afternoon, while Dennis was reacquainting himself with running the cinema, I packed all the film prints into the trunk of my car, along with my belongings: books, clothes, and a vintage Underwood typewriter. Just as I had everything in place and closed the hood, I heard a sound like metal breaking. The key turned freely around in the lock when I tried to re-open the trunk. My belongings were being held hostage by my car!

We hadn't travelled more than a hundred meters from Nyback's home when the exhaust pipe fell out of it's fixture and dragged nosily on the asphalt. We quickly fixed it with some duct tape but, of course, before we were able to locate a hardware store and a more durable repair solution, the duct tape melted under the engine's heat. The guys at a nearby gas station let me borrow a pair of pliers and pointed me in the direction of their garbage container, where I was able to locate a length of wire. My impromptu wire fixture didn't hold out for long, either. In desperation, I tried to rip out the whole exhaust pipe and muffler and just throw it away, but was unable to do so.

I succeeded in fixing the exhaust into place following another attempt with the wire, and out onto the interstate we went.

"Get me to the airport," demanded Pam. "I hate this car. It may get you to San Francisco, but I'm gonna take a rental car. If you want to leave this piece of trash behind, we can split the rental car."

Better to have her out of the car than have her bitching all the way down south, I thought. I would drop her off at the airport and continue alone in my car. After all, I wasn't going to leave it behind with my valuables imprisoned in the trunk.

The closer we got to the airport, the smoother the Dodge ran. And it went even smoother after we found a car rental agency and Pam got off.

I wasn't in too much of a hurry and so took some time to relax — driving slowly down the beautiful coastal highway in short daylight trips, checking out the fascinating vistas of the rocky Oregon and Northern Californian coast, eating big greasy meals in the most antiquated road-side diners I could find, hanging out in rural town bars, and spending my nights in cheap motels, watching wacky TV shows. For a few days it was a vacation, pure and simple; I had made enough money at the Pike Street Cinema to cover my bills and my journey to San Francisco. After that... well, I would find out.

Crossing the Golden Gate Bridge and into San Francisco, I quickly found the way to my host, Jack Stevenson, who was living in the fog enshrouded, largely Chinese, Richmond District of Western San Francisco. Good news was waiting for me — Katrin, an old East German girlfriend of mine was coming over. Our on/off relationship dated back further than my days as a Leipzig gravedigger. In a moment of drunken recklessness, I had sent her a letter from Seattle asking if she wanted to drive with me from San Francisco to New York. I had almost forgotten about it. Now she was on her way.

But first I had my show with Pam at the Commotion Club, a punk venue down in the Mission, the San Franciscan equivalent of New York's East Village. Here the coffee was better however, the Puerto Ricans were replaced by Mexicans, and instead of chain-smoking, black-leather punks with long hair and needle marks up their arms, we had burrito-munching, goatee bearded punks, with rings through every piece of flesh on their face.

It was destined to be one of the worst shows in my life.

I had a locksmith drill open the lock of the trunk in order to gain access to the film prints again. After that I hung out at the club, making phone call after phone call to Pam at her warehouse space — until eventually she got the projection equipment loaded into a car and drove over. The auditorium was already filling up, mainly with punk rockers sporting GG Allin T-shirts and the names of various GG bands scrawled onto their leather jackets. 'Murder Junkies,' 'Jabbers,' 'Drug Whores,' were the inscriptions on every second back that came through the door. The moment Pam arrived we set up the equipment and gave it a test. It all worked — but at an incredibly low level of quality. The sound from both the Super-8 and 16mm projectors were all woolly and the voices barely discernible. The super-8 machine continually lost the loop, allowing the picture to just run by as a high-speed smear. "GG! GG!" the crowd began to yell as local filmmakers I hadn't seen in years popped up to the projection booth to say hello. I just wished they had all stayed at home where they wouldn't have witnessed the embarrassment the show was to become.

We had no choice — we had to start the show with the equipment as it stood. The soundtrack for *Shred of Sex* was abysmally distorted, while both sound and visuals were fucked up on the Super-8 *Fingered* and *Manhattan Love Suicides*. Only *Playboy Voodoo* came out properly, since it was 16mm and the soundtrack was on audio cassette...

Nobody in the auditorium seemed to care about these movies or the messy projection. They just screamed for "GG!" all the way through them. *Hated* was the only movie they were here to see; everything else on the bill simply gave them more time for drugs and beer in preparation for it.

I left Pam with the projectors and ran out to the nearest grocery store to buy some cigarettes. Somebody on the street called after me. The voice was terribly familiar, and I turned around to see Todd Phillips, director of *Hated*.

"You been in there?" I asked him of the theatre.

"Sure," he replied, "you've got a great crowd."

"Yeah. But the worst projection ever," I told him. "Every second in there feels cursed."

"They all paid. So what? They're all morons anyway." Todd shrugged my worries off. "Anyway, I gotta go. Meeting some chick. Have fun."

Todd was right. As awful as the projection was, as soon as *Hated* hit the screen, even the noisiest punk in the audience fell quiet and listened intently to GG's every scrambled word. The club suddenly felt like a church, with a mumbling high priest up on the screen — anything that came out of his mouth was sacred, whatever the condition in which it was transmitted.

Happily and peacefully everyone filed out of the exit when the film had ended. The show made enough money for me to keep going a little while longer.

I helped Pam to pack up her shitty equipment and drove over to the Lower Haight, where Jack had a show with vintage sexploitation playing at some other punk club. When I arrived, the screen was blank, the lights were up and Jack was fumbling with the projector, a screwdriver in his hand. It surely was a damned night...

A few days later, Katrin arrived — happy, horny, and with barely enough cash for a Greyhound ticket should she need to bail out of our drive to distant, distant New York. I showed her around San Francisco for a few days and then off we set, towards desert ghost towns and the Mississippi, destined for the warm welcome of my friends in New York.

Since the speedometer wasn't working, there was no way to tell how *Highway 50* slowly we were creeping through the Utah desert. Suffice it to say, it was slow enough to arouse the suspicion of the Highway Patrol. A cop car passed us by, idled by the side of the road, passed us again, idled by the side of the road, and eventually started to tail us. I could see the officer through my rear-view mirror talking into his handset. I figured he was getting a check on my license plate number.

Katrin got nervous. "The police! What are we gonna do?!"

I regretted having told her that my international driver's license expired a few days ago.

"Well, just stay calm. They aren't gonna hole us up for driving too slow," was the only thing I could say, not quite sure myself if they would. After all, not only had my licensed expired, but the car wasn't insured. If they checked some of it's safety features, they could squeeze us into costly repairs we had no way of affording.

Through a loudspeaker the cop told us to pull off the highway and stop.

I handed him my passport with the expired student visa, my driver's license and papers which I'd got when the car was registered in my name. Bewildered, the cop scrutinised the little multi-language booklet that constituted my international driver's license. He then had another, longer conversation with his headquarters, before handing my papers back.

Smalltown USA.
Austin, Nevada.
Photos: Katrin Krahnstöver

"They are in order," he said, clearly not having been able to fathom my German issued licence. "But what's the matter?" he added. "Why are you driving so slowly? Anything wrong with the car?"

"I would say so," I sighed. "Check it out for yourself."

My front right tire was new and of all the tires was in the best shape.

"That's my reserve wheel," I told him. "I put it on a few miles back after the tire blew. Look at the left one. You see? It's worn down to the point where the wires that hold it together are exposed — that's why I drive so slowly. There must be something wrong with the alignment. I'm hoping I'll be able to make the next town and get some new tires if I drive slow enough. Don't wanna be stuck in the desert."

"You'll be alright," the cop replied. "Keep your speed up. Next town is Delta, about forty miles from here. Ask for Eddy's, that's the repair shop."

The Jesus Car in a cheap garage, Delta, Utah (above) and broken down outside Virginia City, Nevada (below).
Photos: Katrin Krahnstöver

It was dark when we drove into Delta, a small desert town with empty streets and brightly illuminated twenty-four hour superstores. Not a bar in sight. Of course, Eddy's was closed, so we engaged in our typical evening routine of late: we bought some food from one of the superstores, drove into the desert until we found a convenient place to roll out our blankets, had a meal of bread, cheese, salami and whiskey (with country-and-western songs blaring from the radio), fucked into exhaustion and fell asleep under the clear desert sky.

When the heat drew us out from beneath our blankets in the late morning, I made a discovery that wasn't quite so pleasant. Not only was the worn tire threatening to deflate entirely at any given moment, the car was also stuck in the sand. Whenever I put my foot on the gas, the wheels simply spun around on the spot, digging themselves deeper and deeper into the desert. The town was five miles away.

I stopped a road-maintenance truck that happened by and tried to persuade the guys in it to tow us onto the highway.

"Sorry, we can't do that," they said. And I learned the reason why. "They came up with a law against it. The towing companies pushed it through. They argued that we would damage their business if we helped people for free. A few months ago we could have pulled you out, but not now."

I was given a ride to Delta in the road maintenance truck, where I called the AAA. "We will have a tow truck there in half an hour," promised the voice on the other end of the line. For two hours, I tried unsuccessfully to hitchhike back to the car — then the same roadworkers came by and gave me a lift.

Katrin had resigned to waiting, thirsty and out of cigarettes, in the overheated car.

Eventually the tow truck arrived and, back on the highway, we made the drive into Delta.

"The front wheels are totally out of alignment," the guy at Eddy's told me. "Wouldn't be worth trying to fix it." He glanced at my license plates. "You going to New York? You'd better buy another car. We got cheap used ones here, some for as low as 500 bucks."

"Five-hundred? I paid 200 for this one here," I said. "I better hold onto it."

He shook his head in disbelief and went to look for some cheap re-mould tires.

It was with some relief that we finally left behind that Delta desert dump, and got our twisted tourist trip underway once more. Katrin had come to America to enjoy a cross-country road-movie type of drive, and hadn't yet complained that it was more like a Z-grade nerve endurance shocker.

Like so many Europeans, she had arrived with the notion that the San Franciscan coast would look something like *Baywatch* — San Francisco being in California after all. What a disappointment it was for her to encounter fog and freezing waves from the Pacific breaking on the rocks of Marin County! Now, she set her hopes on swimming in the Great Salt Lake, envisioning it to be like the Dead Sea in Israel — a lake with such a high concentration of salt that bathers sit upon it rather than swim through it. Which makes for funny bathing, of course. Not knowing whether it was possible to float upon it or not, I played with this peculiar concept of the Dead Sea while cruising Salt Lake City

in search of a cheap motel.

"In En Gedi, Israel, you have all these American tourists who believe you can actually float on the Dead Sea and read a newspaper," I told Katrin. "Of course it doesn't work, but they strive to maintain the illusion... the myth. The fat, balding husband struggles in the water with a wet newspaper in his hands, smiling and trying desperately to look relaxed, as the wife captures it all on camera for the loved ones at home. Most end up re-shooting the scene, with the guy sitting on the ground in some puddle somewhere."

We found our cheap motel and the following morning headed out to the beach. Salt Lake City, as the name would imply, has a famous beach resort — Saltair, a huge palace dating back to the 1890s. In spite of its grand restoration, the impressive building was host to nothing more than a few sandwich stands and an exhibition on how great and lively the place was at the turn of the twentieth-century. The reason for its decline and present empty state became clear the closer we walked to the water. The beach was a green, pungent swamp, covered in rot-

The main Mormon temple, Salt Lake City, Utah (top), and plaster replica of seventeenth-century Danish Jesus sculpture.

Previous page: The Jesus Car breaks down in Utah.
Photos: Katrin Krahnstöver

ting seaweed and countless numbers of flies, hovering ready to attack the unfortunate visitor. *I knew, where I had seen this place before!* The Saltair had been the creepily dilapidated beach palace in the 1960 horror classic *Carnival of Souls*, in which the souls of the dead came to dance. The film was shot way before the building had undergone its restoration.

Undeterred, we checked the map and decided to give the little hamlet at the end of a straight desert road a shot — maybe the beach was more inviting there? In our vivid imaginations, we anticipated it to be a place with a lone ice cream parlour and a couple of wooden shacks, surrounded by an unspoiled coast.

We drove thirty miles through dry fields to arrive at the gates of that "hamlet" — it turned out to be a factory where they extracted magnesium from the water in the lake.

Road near Moab, Utah.
Photo: Katrin Krahnstöver

We went back to town and joined a Mormon sightseeing tour. A pale-faced girl showed us the temple sites. The main temple itself however, remained closed to non-believers. The major artefact in the whole tour was a plaster replica of a seventeenth-century Danish Jesus sculpture, located in a concrete building with neon lights. I wasn't impressed.

The 70mm Mormon propaganda movie *Legacy*, on the other hand, which detailed the Mormon trek West under the holy guidance of Joseph Smith and Brigham Young, was quite a professional production. Disappointingly professional actually, slickly circumventing all the campiness displayed in Mormon films of the sixties, films which actually seemed much better suited to what they had to say about their religion. Dennis Nyback had a whole collection of morality thumping flicks, like *How Do I Love Thee?* and *For Time and Eternity*. According to them, eternal damnation was the least Katrin and I could expect for our whiskey-soaked evenings and nightly shenanigans.

America, the celluloid country. No place of any significance hasn't been featured in, or served as location for some movie or another. The bizarre rock formations around Moab in the Canyonlands of Southeast Utah, where we went next, had been host to more than their fair share of film crews, and the local tourist office even published a map indicating the exact shooting locations for more than thirty pictures. Here John Wayne had had gun fights, John Ford had guided settlers, and

Marion Eaton had roamed the deserts as a vampire grandmother in *Sundown*. All in all, I felt a little closer to doomed Barry Newman racing his Dodge Challenger in *Vanishing Point* — available in the 'local' section of the Moab video store. Newman had sped West, chased by cops, on the same Highway 50 we were using to go East. He met with one or two problems before crashing headlong into a police roadblock, but at least Newman could count on the reliability of his car. We couldn't.

In Virginia City, Nevada, the friggin' freeze plug had fallen out again. AAA had towed us to Reno, where a guy in a repair shop refused to install another plug made of rubber. We had no choice but to let him replace it with a metal one — thus, greatly diminishing our budget. Than the stupid problem with the tire... I wasn't about to embark on a trip further South, into Arizona and New Mexico, as Katrin wanted, enticed by the colourful rocks and canyons depicted in her tourist guide book. If we didn't make it to New York soon, I impressed upon her, we would never make it. Besides, all these unforeseen expenses were already forcing us to dip into our gasoline budget.

Aching in first gear for mile upon mile, the car climbed the Rockies and over the Monarch Pass. We found a place to rest for the night near Canyon City, Colorado, which was almost paradise. Surrounded by snow-covered mountains, we parked the car beside an old tree whose branches served as shelter for us. A perfectly clear stream glistened, and there was free refreshment to be had in the plentiful berry bushes. There were even a few cactus plants to commiserate Katrin on having to forgo the cactus gardens of New Mexico.

It was down to earth with a bump come the morning, however, when I discovered that both tires were worn down to the wire again. We were going through tires like gasoline it seemed and so decided to stock up on them at the cheapest place we could find.

I took a gamble and drove another sixty miles to reach an inexpensive repair shop. While we drank weak coffee at a diner, I had the garage check out the alternatives. "Seven-hundred-and-fifty bucks for all the necessary alignment work," they said, "or a bunch of used tires for five bucks a piece." Naturally we went for the latter and stacked as many of the things as we could onto the back seats.

Fresh tires on the wheels, a full tank of gas, and a fresh bottle of whiskey — our spirits were up again. Katrin discovered a large reservoir lake on the map, close to our highway, in the flat grasslands of Eastern Colorado. We arrived to find we were alone, and so camped beside the water, swam naked and fucked all day under the warm September sun.

The night proved less comfortable. A cold wind blew down from the Rockies and we shivered, clutching each other and our blankets tight lest either one be wrenched away.

In the early morning it started to rain. We got up quickly and threw our stuff into the car. I was winding the driver-side window up when it suddenly stopped halfway and slid back down. It disappeared out of sight within the unreachable cavity of the door, despite my continued winding. At least the heating system still worked.

We heard later that day, from a TV in a café, that Canyon City was covered with snow. Sleeping outdoors was out of the question now. Under a rainy sky, we made it through the cattle fields of Kansas, and reached a trashy motel in a town called Mexico, Missouri. We had been quite low on gas when we pulled in, and by morning the car didn't want to start at all. Fortunately the motel was situated right alongside a gas station. Unfortunately, the old guy running the gas station (and tire change shop), had no container he could lend to me with which I could carry gas to my car. I found some plastic cups, but before I was able to make the short distance back to the vehicle, the gas had eaten through the plastic and was on the floor. In a garbage can I found a bottle — this would give me enough gas to drive the car around to the pumps, I thought. It should have. But the car still didn't move.

Suddenly, an unshaven fat guy drove over in a pick-up truck, his elderly mother with bleached hairdo and heavy make-up next to him. "Need any help?" he asked. "Well, I don't think it's a lack of gas", I said, "but the car isn't doing anything." The guy dropped from his pick-up, popped the hood of my car and started to fumble around with the engine.

Rockies near Monarch Pass.
Photos: Katrin Krahnstöver

We checked out the battery, the air filter, and whatever else we could get our hands on, the guy's mother looking on curious. Neither of us had a clue as to what the matter might be, and I was getting ready to give the AAA another call when the guy suddenly had a brainstorm. "It's the ventilation clap," he said. "You need some spray to keep it

moving the right way. I'll drive you to a store where you can get it."

He did and the spray worked. Accepting no thanks, the guy and his mother drove off in their pick-up, leaving me with a working car and the cheapest repair job ever. "You are so damn lucky," Katrin told me, "but never before the very last minute."

We hadn't driven into Denver, we bypassed Kansas City, but St Louis was a city that Katrin wanted to see. And besides, with the Mississippi river flooded — the 'flooding of the century' as the papers called it — only St Louis offered a working bridge to cross.

We came into town from the Northwest, only to enter a giant ghetto of ruined buildings and young black gangs hanging out on street corners. We kept on going. The city didn't change until we reached downtown, where the vast empty streets and grey skies reminded me a lot of Detroit. Neither of us felt much like hanging around and so we quickly traversed the bridge in order to find a rural motel in Illinois.

Katrin had attended too many jazz festivals to forget about St Louis entirely, however. We went back and spent the entire following day visiting the inner city. They have a huge steel structure there called the Gateway Arch, twice as high as the Statue of Liberty, or so a sign claimed. I remembered a story I had read somewhere: a guy had tried to walk over the arch while his wife filmed him — only to record on video how he had fallen to his death when the wind blew him off.

It was freezing cold, nothing going on. The bars were expensive, the jazz clubs were out of our financial reach, and, to cap it all off, the exhibition at the visitor centre informed us that St Louis was a much more lively place in the forties. I believed it. Their once bustling train station, the busiest in the whole mid-west, was now a shopping centre.

Still, it was better than the train station in Detroit, which was just a ruin.

East of the Rockies, west of New York, the so-called Heartland was a rotten mess of boredom and decline, poverty and instant coffee. Middle America began to feel like a vast and borderless East Germany.

Downtown St Louis, Missouri.
Photo: Katrin Krahnstöver

Eastward we travelled. East was all we wanted right now. Two days from St Louis and we crossed the border into New York State, the tire stack on our backseats having depleted considerably and my side window still lost in the door's murky interior.

Niagara Falls was the last of our tourist sites. I felt almost home being surrounded by cars with New York license plates, supermarkets that offered the widest variety of food we'd seen since we left San Francisco, and people who appeared to be able to tell the difference between cappuccino and chop suey.

The Falls where an overcrowded nightmare — fat mamas with their obnoxious brats at every turn, overweight pensioners on every park bench, and jocks with their giggling cheerleader girlfriends leaning over every inch of railing. All of whom were probably staying in one of the illuminated high-rise hotels which gave the Falls the appearance of being a part of some sprawling urban park.

We slept in the car that night — for the first and only time. Vietnamese cage prisons could hardly have been less comfortable.

The morning saw us back at the Falls, with me idling among the tourists on the American side and Katrin going to Canada. I couldn't possibly accompany her, as my expired student visa would have left me trapped over there. As soon as she got back, we headed out of town and toward the New York Thruway.

On our right wheel was a winter tire with a thick profile. Amazingly, it had no latticework of wire holding it together, as I'd come to expect, just a mesh of white threads. By this point in our journey, I well knew that tires were durable, and even with the wire poking through it was still possible to ride on them for another 100 miles or so. We had no decent spare tires left, only one damaged one. I counted the miles to New York City and calculated that another new tire would leave us with less than twenty bucks. Would the winter tire get us to New York? Unlikely, but we could try running it till it blew. Suddenly we hit thirty miles of road repair, and the decision was made for us. Concrete slabs narrowed the highway making it impossible to stop without creating a traffic jam. The tire would break at any minute, I was convinced. Then came a sign which read: 'Road Works For Next Ten Miles.' I raced ahead as fast as I could (driving slowly did nothing to preserve worn tires, as I learned in the Utah desert). The concrete slabs were gone, the highway opened up its full width — and the tire broke at that very moment.

Lucky at the last minute.

I steered the car to the side of the road and replaced the useless tire with a slightly less useless one I held in reserve. It wouldn't get us far, that was for sure, and a quick change in a repair shop at the next town left us with nine dollars.

The Tappan Sea Bridge over the Hudson had a crowded toll station. Tens of thousands of cars travelled through it daily. Yet, the toll collector went out of his way to inform me that my "engine sounds darn bad. Goin' to the city? Then, good luck."

We paid him our four bucks and crossed the river.

New York. The Bronx. In case of another tire breakdown, we could take the subway from here.

Harlem.

The FDR Drive along the East River.

Forty-second Street. I counted each highway exit we passed as a big success. Each exit brought us closer to our destination!

Thirty-fourth Street!

Twenty-third Street!

Fourteenth Street!

Houston — our exit! We could walk from here if necessary.

Driving East.

Avenue C.

Avenue A.

First Avenue.

To the right.

A left again.

First Street — up to the middle of the block.

The lights were on at Petra and Cord's place. We had made it — with five bucks between us to spare.

Before my departure to the West, I had lived in a NYU dormitory. Which meant that now, upon my return to the city, I was homeless. Katrin had another week left before her flight home. Petra and Cord let us stay at their place that night, but we had to be out the next day as they were expecting visitors from Germany.

I had to find some accommodation quickly.

I spent the day calling people all over town and leaving messages on answer machines. Finally, I got through to Alyce Wittenstein in person. "Subatomic Productions. Hello."

Hi, this is Johannes, back to New York

"Welcome back!" Alyce was pleased to hear from me. "You've got to come over and see our rough cut of *The Deflowering*. Those shots with you are great."

I had been a production assistant and extra for Alyce's latest sci-fi picture.

"Yeah, I will," I told her. "But I'm actually calling because me and my girlfriend need a place to stay."

"Let me ask Steve. *Steve!*" I heard her yelling.

Steve Ostringer, Alyce's boyfriend and co-producer, had a house out in South Ozone Park, Queens, near JFK Airport. It turned out that we could stay there for as long as we wanted. Steve was over at Alyce's most of the time anyway.

After sleeping outdoors, in cramped motels and the car, we suddenly had a whole house to ourselves. It was a old wooden structure in a quiet street.

"The area looks safer than it is," Steve said of the neighbourhood in which he lived. "Don't leave anything in the car, though."

Well, I never would anyway — I couldn't close the window, after all. Last night in Alphabet City, I had expected to find a sleeping bum on the backseat when I returned to the car. It didn't happen.

Prop car for Alyce Wittenstein's *The Deflowering.* New York City
Photo: Katrin Krahnstöver

Neither did it happen in South Ozone Park, but the first morning there brought an entirely different twist. I couldn't get the car to start. Undeterred, I got my spray out, opened the hood, and found that the battery was gone.

"You hadn't secured it with a chain?" queried Steve. "That's what everybody does around here."

Steve happened to have a spare battery in the basement, and advised me to buy a chain and a lock right away. I did.

To reach Manhattan, it took a forty-minute drive down Atlantic Avenue and through the heart of Bedford-Stuyvesant. In the day time, whenever I hit a red light, squeegee men would smear my windshield with dirty foaming water and kick the car as I drove off without handing them a dollar. At night, Atlantic Avenue was deserted and the chop shops and muffler stations lining the street were locked down tight. Ragged bums and dope dealers with white sneakers were its only population after dark. Alyce kept on warning me against driving down Atlantic Avenue at night — not in my unreliable car anyway. Being stranded there was certainly an uncomfortable prospect, but hey, it was the shortest route.

I was drinking Rolling Rock at the Max Fish bar on Ludlow Street one night with Katrin, when suddenly the door burst open and in stormed a very happy-looking Jeri Rossi.

"I saw my car outside and the hood still felt warm! It's still working!" she shouted in delight. "It got you to the West Coast and back?! *Incredible!*"

We gave Jeri a lift to a gallery opening in the Meat District, and she fondled the car all the way. "My car! It's still alive..."

The day of Katrin's departure arrived and we started out early. Through Brooklyn, over the Manhattan Bridge, through downtown, the Lincoln Tunnel — I was happy with every landmark that got us closer to the New Jersey Turnpike, and ultimately Newark Airport.

Katrin was relieved that she'd survived these few weeks.

With Katrin gone and their visitors having also departed, I moved in with Petra and Cord and started my job at the Millennium Film Workshop again — which was just a three-minute walk away from the apartment.

Time to get rid of the car.

I phoned my way through the junkyard listings in the Yellow Pages.

"A seventy-three Dodge Dart? Don't bother. Stay away with that one," was the general response I got. The highest offer I received was thirty-five dollars from a scrap metal dealer on Rockaway Avenue in East New York. I snapped it up.

The journey there was the last for the Jesus car.

Ten minutes after arriving at the scrapyard, I had in my pocket the thirty-five bucks cash. With the battery in hand and the license plates under my arm, I walked away casting a couple of last glances at the grey, bulky, unreliable and... beloved heap. I wandered through the ghetto until I found a bus station. People on the bus and those later on the subway made sure that they kept a safe distance from me and my acid-spilling battery.

As a last relic of the Dodge and our journey across country, the battery rested under Petra and Cord's kitchen table for a few weeks.

Until Steve eventually came by to reclaim it.

The Home-Movie Madhouse

The young man with the horn-rimmed glasses, his blonde hair trimmed to a crew-cut, laughed into the bobbing camera as he ventured down the sunny lake-side promenade of a Swiss resort town. He ran towards the camera, his hands grabbing for it, whereupon the scene shook violently — fast pans from left to right, swirling up over the Alps and lake. Suddenly the focus of the camera was on a girl wearing a grey trenchcoat and sunglasses, a silk knotted scarf on her head. She too was laughing. Across the busy lake-side street the camera captured several passing fifties' model Mercedes and Volkswagen, before returning again to the girl's happy face.

The picture faded to white, and remained white for almost a minute.

I left the little 8mm reel on my transfer projector running. Images slowly began to materialise again, but not this time of lakes and Alps and girlfriends — here was something else entirely. The guy in the film had evidently taken his movie camera off to the war in Korea, but hadn't bothered to change the reel before starting to document the carnage over there. Following his playful interlude in Switzerland came burning jeeps. Then, motionless mangled soldiers sprawled on the ground, their limbs bent into grotesque shapes. One soldier was missing his head... The picture faded back to white, from which faint grey, hardly discernible, shadows emerged, and a barely recognisable Army

Photo:
Silke Mayer

Field Medicine Camp. A few scratches danced over the monitor screen, then the reel was over.

I pressed the rewind button on the VCR and spooled the film back on the projector, glancing at the other monitors: on the Super-8 monitor a little boy wearing an oversize cap on his head shovelled sand into a plastic toy bucket on a crowded summer beach; on the 16mm monitor a naked woman danced through a forest clearing, reflecting the clouds in a big mirror which she balanced in her hands — a one-minute shot that ran on for fifteen minutes with its numerous different takes. I'd better watch out with this one. It was part of an exercise in 'art', and the art people were already swift to complain about the quality of the transfers — whenever the image came out too dark or too pink, for instance, or when the projector stumbled over one of their many bad splices, lost the loop, and resulted in the picture momentarily vanishing in a race of blurring colour.

It was all inclined to happen here at New York's indisputably cheapest film-to-video transfer shop, equipped with suitably shabby technical gear.

Rafik's was the name of the place, a store situated a block south of Union Square on a less fashionable stretch of Broadway, which catered to downtown filmmakers. It sold film cleaner, splicing tape, take-up reels and the like from a long glass counter in a windowless corridor. Hidden in the back where the two transfer rooms. The larger one, replete with natural light, was used for video-to-video; the windowless little cubicle next to it was where I fiddled with the transfers of film-to-video.

The grey metal shelves on my walls were overflowing with plastic bags and cardboard boxes, filled to the hilt with films waiting to be processed. By far the majority of these were Super-8 and 8mm home movies from the fifties and sixties, tiny stickers labelling the reels 'Summer 1956', 'Susan's Birthday Party 1962', 'Christmas 1968' or some such.

It was the Christmas season of 1995, and the concept of giving memories as gifts was high in festive demand. Grandchildren would find boxes containing vintage film rolls in their grandparents' attic — films that nobody had seen for twenty or so years, not since the broken projector was thrown into the trash anyway. Now, they were being revived on video.

The nostalgia-drenched family gatherings anticipated by my customers caused my head to spin. Not knowing anybody in these bygone celluloid images, most of the home movies looked interchangeable to me. White middle class families spending their summer days on some lake or beach. Kids swimming, kids playing in the sand, father preparing the barbecue, daughters jumping from the springboard into a pool, friends and neighbours water-skiing and playing waterball. Water, water, water… over and over, from one reel to the next, an endless fusion of water-related pictures.

Often I played several films on the monitors at the same time to wallow in the inanity of it all. People it seemed shot nothing but their happiest days, which invariably were those spent over at the lake. Family parties were the next predictable category — albeit falling some way behind the aquatic leader.

Occasionally amongst the flood of bathing suits and Bermuda shorts, I would find a bizarre treasure. Just a few days ago I had a couple of Super-8 reels from the early seventies to transfer, labelled 'Long Dong Silver' and featuring a black guy with an incredibly large penis, its tip dangling down to his knees. Grinning awkwardly, he walked naked through a gaudy Hawaiian set, shaking his hips to propel the oversized sausage between his legs into pathetic motion. A bevy of scantily clad girls danced around him. It was a freak show — Long Dong swanking around to a barrage of salacious comments made by a black guy wearing an Afro haircut, silver-rimmed sunglasses and thick rings on his fingers.

"Look, Honky! Look at what Long Dong has got for your wife!"

He might have yelled this, but I couldn't tell for sure — the films had no soundtrack.

One of the girls working the desk had wandered into my booth and seen the lolloping oversized appendage on the monitor. She was out in a second, returning swiftly with the whole Rafik's crew. They stretched their necks in my tiny workshop to catch a glimpse of the huge dick. As long as the Long Dong Silver movies were running, the customers in the shop had to wait.

"Is that for real?" the girls asked excitedly. "How can somebody have such a piece of meat down there?" They deduced that Long Dong could never achieve an erection, and that it "Must be fake anyway".

Long Dong might indeed have struggled to achieve an erection, but fake?

"Hey, people are born with two heads or with a third arm sticking out of their back," I countered the accusation. "Compared to that, Long Dong is almost normal."

Frank, the shop's skinny gopher, brought the matter into historical perspective and reasoned that Long Dong had figured prominently in the Thomas Clarence/Anita Hill sex-harassment court hearings of 1991. Nobody cared. When the films were over, the girls moved in on me: "You get porn or sex-type stuff here often?" they giddily inquired. "Let us know whenever something comes up!"

It was obvious Rafik, the owner, wasn't around. The fifty-something Palestinian refugee had started the place in the 1960s as a venue for

underground film shows. When that ceased to make money, he converted the space into the shop it was now. Rafik would invite his college kid employees to generous parties one day, and perhaps fire them the next, depending on how his quickly shifting mood took him.

Today, Rafik was sitting at his desk. It wasn't one of his good days. I could hear him yelling at the staff through my closed door. I had never had a bad experience with Rafik myself, so didn't worry too much about his tantrums. Indeed, when I told him that the Christmas orders were too many to process within regular shop hours, he pitched in, and we hung out together until midnight, plowing through the orders, drinking red wine, and musing over the strangest stuff flickering across the screens... Rafik was shaken by *Executions*, a British documentary presenting images of capital punishment from around the world. We talked about the underground movies he used to run, and the underground shows I was involved in. I sensed he respected me for what I was doing outside of my hours at his place. The people behind the desks however, they never knew if they would be looking for another job an hour after they arrived in the morning.

The pseudo-Cocteau mirror scenes on the 16mm projector were finally over, and I quickly threaded in the next film. Sixteen millimetre was the format of choice for the artists and also the standard for home movies from the thirties and forties. With 16mm there was always the possibility of coming across something of interest. On my first day at Rafik's, I was given a 16mm home movie from 1937 to transfer. The only colour remaining on the emulsion were shades of silver — a shimmering silver Kansas horse farm, with a shimmering silver black Ford zooming by on the highway. "I'm gonna see America's hidden history here," I had thought to myself at that moment. And of course, that's precisely what I did end up witnessing, day in, day out at Rafik's: fringe history, up close and personal, courtesy of family movies with the occasional hair stuck in the camera gate.

What do we have here? A lump of dirt on a grey carpet floor — it looks like dog shit. A hand reaches into shot, picks it up and turns it over to reveal that it's actually a dog shit novelty item made of clay with a $2.90 price tag.

I had seen shots like this before. They belonged to a guy hired to produce a commercial for a novelty shop. His first thirty takes of that scene evidently weren't good enough — now I had a whole second batch comprising of another twenty minutes.

Water-skiing on Super-8, kids in oversized swimming trunks at a beach on 8mm, and Rafik yelling insults at his staff outside my cubicle.

Photo: Silke Mayer

Time for a bite from my pastrami sandwich and a gulp of coffee from the styrofoam cup resting on the metal shelf.

Rafik got louder and louder, but it wasn't clear at whom he was shouting. "Surrounded by idiots," he barked. "I'm employing morons!"

Was Frank the focus of Rafik's wrath? Frank who would tell me five times a day that it was "better to work smart than to work hard," stealing a momentary respite in my cubicle when he should have been carrying heavy boxes of video tapes upstairs? Or Susan, the girl from Baghdad, daughter of Iraqi refugees, who had grown up in Leipzig, East Germany — the same city as me? Susan told me that Rafik's vicious verbal assaults sometimes reduced her to tears. Or was it Gina, the fanatical non-smoker, ill at ease in an environment where cigarettes burned from ashtrays on every available surface?

I didn't venture to find out. Instead, back to my monitors where more water activity was unfolding, and that hand reached down once again for the brown novelty item.

Until a few weeks ago, I had been working as a 'monitor', overseeing the activities at the Millennium Film Workshop on East 4th Street. Though more an avant-garde workshop, it also happened to be host to a home movie maker by the name of Ron Ellis. In one of the little editing rooms, Ellis had spliced into a film the fragments of his life — the culmination of a year of painstaking work on the workshop's tiny splicing console. After he was done he showed me the result. The film started with Ellis very much in the era of *Scorpio Rising*, hanging out with a Brooklyn biker gang. It shifted in and out of family life, drug parties and shots of changing Brooklyn neighbourhoods. There followed outtakes from a short film Ellis had made with his mongoloid sister in the eighties, for which he had won an Academy Award for Best Short Film. The film ended with Ellis and Telly Savalas on a Hollywood stage.

Ellis told me about the offers from Hollywood that came in quick and fast after his Academy Award, but that he wasn't interested in a system he believed would exploit him and ultimately reject him. Instead, he took the next plane out of town... and spent ten years in India as personal projectionist for a Guru.

Too bad he hadn't any film from this era of his life.

There was a knock on my door and Dorothy came in, a tiny black girl. "More work for you," she quipped, still smirking in disbelief at the memory of Long Dong Silver. She left a large plastic bag on my table, the accompanying order sheet stating that its contents were for 'Video to audio transfer'. I took the first tape from the bag and placed it in the VCR. The picture of an old man appeared, seated at a plastic table. He began to talk about day-to-day Jewish life in 1930s Poland. I realised I was watching a story I had read about in *The New York Times* — the video was part of an endeavour by a Steven Spielberg-financed Jewish organisation, which aimed to collate every detail of Jewish existence before and during the Holocaust. Hundreds of hours of interviews had been shot on film, according to the report. And now here it all was, on my desk, waiting to be transferred to audio tape! In the next few weeks, I would have a soundtrack of pain-wracked voices relating how loved ones were taken from their homes and work places and sent to the gas chamber.

I started the recording. *"In 1938, we were living in a town called Sochaczew..."*

Meanwhile the Super-8 reel had run out, freeing up another job. I threaded in a fresh one: more family scenes, this time courtesy of a company called Manhattan Video. When the first such order had come in, I was a little mystified — Manhattan Video was a video rental store. Were they picking up home movies on flea markets, having them transferred to video and stacking the results in a 'Home Movies' section on their shelves, ready to be rented? Why would anybody want to rent such films? I reasoned that perhaps some customers needed to fabricate a safe middle-class background, for the possible intention of impressing prospective in-laws. After all, better to give the illusion of a glorious youth spent at the seaside (kids in home movies all look the same), rather than admit to the reality of having been brought up in, say, a trailer park.

Rafik had enlightened me: Manhattan Video wasn't into that kind of deception. They simply subcontracted Rafik's to transfer films handed in at their Midtown shops.

Elsewhere, Super-8 jungle footage as shot from an airplane played. A village. Asia, Vietnam or perhaps Cambodia. Sans soundtrack, rockets were fired in silence from someplace beneath the camera, cutting a trail of smoke through the air. They impacted on the grass-covered huts far below, blowing them apart in mute destruction. The whole thing looked completely removed from reality, as if the scenario was unfolding in Toyland. With the village in smoke, the plane continued its unerring trajectory across the jungle tree-tops. Other planes, four or five of them, dropped into the picture, releasing thick white clouds over the trees. Agent Orange? I was in no position to tell for sure, but I assumed it wasn't fertiliser...

A knock on the door and Dave walked in, an apprentice of a few days who was being taught video-to-video transfer. He was learning fast, Rafik had told me.

"Just wanted to say good bye," Dave said to my surprise. "I'm fired."

"Huh? Why?" I asked.

"I showed a customer the transfer results on a monitor and Rafik freaked out," Dave explained. "That wasn't my business, Rafik told me;

talking to the customers was off-limits to me."

I was bewildered, and told him I talked to customers all the time with Rafik around. Dave shouldered his bag and shrugged. "Well, this was my time at Rafik's! See you around."

Dave closed the door behind him.

Gina had been training him and she herself was leaving tomorrow. Where would Rafik find anyone at such short notice to take their place? His problem. Rafik could be nuts, and didn't always seem to be thinking straight. Yet, at his most choleric, he could pick up the ringing phone and answer in his most charming voice — "Hello, Rafik's. With what can I help you?" — only to return to his screaming fit the moment he hung up.

Time to change the audio tape for the Holocaust recording. The same old man was still recounting his youth. Had the Germans invaded his town yet? I hadn't been listening. His voice had become a part of the environment; a general background noise along with the grinding of the projectors.

"I had an uncle who was running a jewellery business..."

I listened to him as I made the switch.

"I became an apprentice of his..."

A family on faded 8mm went to a mountain and started hiking. The Vietnam footage on the Super-8 monitor had been followed by a lengthy college party, underexposed to the point that at times it was almost black, accompanied by horribly distorted seventies rock music on the film's magnetic track.

'MM Serra' read the name tag on the next 16mm reel. I knew her. She was the head of the New York Filmmaker's Coop, and a dedicated filmmaker when it came to promoting the pleasures of lesbian SM.

A few months ago, I had arranged for her a tour of European art cinemas — a tour that started off a disaster. The day she was supposed to arrive in Amsterdam, she called me in Copenhagen, where I was showing some American Underground films at a festival. Yelling hysterically into the handset, she told me that she hadn't yet left JFK airport, that all the films in her programme — 'Coming to Power: Sexually Explicit Films by Women Artists' — had been stolen from the luggage compartment of the Carey bus she took from Manhattan. I cancelled her first two shows while she returned to New York to try and find replacement prints of the lost films. Or, on failing that, substituting them with similar-themed alternatives. There followed two days of hectic calls between New York and Copenhagen, with me acting as Serra's counsellor — calming her down as much as I could, trying to keep her in a constructive mood, and being an advisor for alternatives. I also had the task of calling all the cinemas involved with the tour and relaying the news that the films in their schedules for the show were now wrong. On the third day, I met Serra in Hanover. Her show at the Kommunales Kino was at once a huge success, but with an edgy dismissive undercurrent courtesy of short-haired feminists unable to draw anything positive from the scenes of fucking, sucking and general kinkiness.

From there, she went on to ten or twelve other cities, a travelling messenger for the New York sex scene.

Yesterday, she had arrived at my cubicle (gazing in awe at the Andy Warhol Screen Test which happened to be playing — a young man reading aloud a revolutionary statement). She asked me to take special care in the transfer of her newest picture, *Soimême*. *Soimême* was a document of Goddess Rosemary masturbating on stage at some performance space, sprinkling the carpet with piss upon climaxing. (It wasn't piss to Serra, but "female ejaculate".) It was material that the desk girls would loved to have seen... except today they had Rafik's scrutinising eyes to contend with.

Gina came into my booth.

"I'm fired," she said.

"Why?"

"Don't know," she replied.

"So, Rafik has to do the transfers himself now, since there's nobody left," I laughed.

"Looks like it. I told him that tomorrow was my last day anyway. Fuck him."

"You got a better job?"

"No, I just can't stand it here anymore. Something will come up. At least now you'll be able to smoke yourself to death. Nobody left to bitch about it anymore."

"I never cared anyway. As you know," I grinned.

Sure enough, the next time I saw Rafik he was running around with a stack of video tapes in his arms, hurrying to feed them into the transfer machines. His yelling and shouting had stopped — he hadn't the time for that now.

Back at the Holocaust transfer, an old woman was talking in Yiddish. I could have understood some of it if I listened intently enough. But I didn't.

What was happening with the Super-8? A Christmas party in a suburban home, personal and homely — not worth looking at. The 8mm? The same guy on the hiking trip. His subject matter hadn't got any better, having since moved his family to the inevitable lakeside. His camera technique had improved, however, and he was composing his shots with some care, focusing, checking the light, and keeping dirt out of the gate. This guy had talent! If he had just made a little more effort and done some editing, injected some humour, or even created a story and got his kids to act! Better still, if only he'd turned the camera onto his daily life instead of just vacations...

A knock on the door snapped me out of my ruminations. It was Dave, grinning. "I'm back!" he laughed. "Rafik just called me — I'm hired again! He needs someone to run his equipment. Can't do it all himself. I even get paid for the time I was away. It's as if nothing had happened!" Whistling, Dave disappeared to the video room.

Rafik himself had left only a few minutes earlier, probably seeking quiet respite following his hectic two hours manning the video transfers. I wandered over to the front desk, where Frank, Dorothy and the other two girls who worked there looked particularly despondent. 'HELP CONSTANTLY WANTED' read a hand-written cardboard sign. Many a struggling young filmmaker who stopped by at Rafik's for a can of Dust-Off also left a résumé, just in case something should turn up. It usually did, but rarely for anything more taxing or creative than re-placing one of the clerks.

The air of despondency over the desk was countered by Dave's faintly discernible whistling. The front door opened — and suddenly up bobbed the clerks' heads. Was it Rafik returning? No, just a customer. Their faces returned to expressions of impenetrable introspection. They wanted nothing more than to be left alone until it was time to shut up shop. These were employees Rafik could easily replace — a fact which for them Dave's returning had somehow inflamed.

I thought I was going to make their day: I had some porn on my 16mm projector. But watching porn was suddenly not so high on their agenda.

I went back to watch it alone. The porn comprised of a home-made brew from the Lower East Side, circa early seventies. Whether or not the name of the director on the print was genuine I couldn't have said, but I suspected that the name of the lead actress was for real — it was the same name as the customer who dropped the job off for transfer-ring, and whose name appeared on the job tag. A mother, perhaps even grandmother, eager to relive the transgressions of her youth.

The film was set in a sparsely furnished Lower East Side apartment, with the typical multiple cross-shaped lattice work over the window. A naked couple both with dark blonde hair faced one another: he had sideburns and greasy hair that fell over his ears; she had breasts that stood out sharply. They embraced. He fondled her tits. They kissed. They dropped down to a mattress on the floor and unceremoniously began to fuck.

Throughout, a monotonous voice on the soundtrack counted out numbers. *"One, two, three... twenty, twenty-one... forty-five, forty-six..."* It lent to the proceedings a distinctly artificial feel.

These people were making a statement!

The camera made the occasional quick cut from one position to the next. But always remained at a distance, resolutely refusing to zoom in. The impression was that of a casual observer, who didn't really want to get too involved.

All the while, the off-screen voice coldly recited its numbers.

The couple on the mattress crawled from one position to another —

him on top, her on top, sideways, doggy-style, their bodies shimmering with sweat. The bright sunlight that poured through the bars of the window cast rhombus patterns over the apartment.

The numbers suddenly ceased being spoken out aloud, and switched instead to digits that appeared in the right hand corner of the screen. Their place on the soundtrack was taken over by the couple's groans and heavy breathing. His actions became more pronounced the longer the sex lasted, and her gasping slipped from a loud staccato into a long scream.

Clinically detached from the unfolding scenario, negating completely the efforts of the couple on the mattress, the numbers continued to flash. They could fuck themselves to death — it wouldn't halt or impede

Photo: Silke Mayer

the onscreen tally.

The girl in the film finally reached climax, howling at the top of her voice and scratching bloody marks into the guy's back with her fingernails. She relaxed and stretched out her arms. The guy continued thrusting into her, until he too came. The numbers vanished. The girl got up and walked out of frame. The guy sat on the mattress, staring languorously beyond the camera. The End.

This certainly wasn't the movie to lift spirits, and I was glad not to have had the clerks there to watch it after all. It felt like it had been fished from a time capsule, a film made in the days when sex was considered a tool for relaying even the most drab of messages.

I noted the telephone number of the 'actress' in the film. Maybe some day I would call her to try and book the print for one of my underground shows. Maybe she would even agree to appear as a 'special guest'? The film would go well with other gritty period pieces, like, say, *A Day in the Death of Danny D*, the 1965 Harlem-lensed account of a junkie's demise. Or even the dark homosexual porn of Curt McDowell's *Loads*. Together, those three movies could make quite a sinister show — assuaged perhaps by a couple of less depressing five-minute pieces. How about some of Otto Mühl's Material Action films as well? Hell, yeah! I wanted to start building the show there and then, scheduling another night of nihilistic depravity at the Limbo Café or the Knitting Factory!

Excited, and pumped full of fresh ideas, I turned off my equipment. Six-thirty. The shop was closing. No overtime today!

Snow was falling thick and heavy when I stepped out of Rafik's and into the night. It capped the many tips of Grace Church and had turned the streets into a soft mush, all white except for the pale yellow reflection of streetlights and the golden hue of Broadway in winter.

I headed east, towards the Korean Barbecue on 9th Street, to fry squid in the company of that Japanese girl with the deep brown eyes I'd met a few days ago...

Suicide Cinema

The setting: a luxurious Southern mansion. Smiling insecurely, the girl with thick black hair was perched on a bed covered by a tiger skin rug, deep scratches in the emulsion running through the image. Its tail wagging, a Doberman trotted towards her. Her cue. Now smiling broadly, the girl grabbed the dog, played with him, kissed him on the nose and took his penis in her hands. Close-up — and for a few brief moments the image was lost to a cacophony of distortion. The chemical makeup of the celluloid had begun to decompose and created blotches, which rolled madly around the screen. When the unspooling picture became visible again, the girl had her skirt raised and the dog was licking her pussy. She clearly wasn't happy; desperation and disgust were etched on her face.

"Where did you say you found these movies?" I asked the red-bearded man seated next to me. We were up in the tiny projection booth of the ramshackle Lower East Side movie house, watching the film through the look-out. The guy took a long sip from his can of Budweiser, and explained. "All the films I brought in came from the one toolbox. I'm a dealer of antiques and oddities at flea markets. I go to all sorts of places to find stuff that I can sell to the Manhattan hipsters. One day, I was up in Harlem when it started to rain. I dashed into the nearest place I could find — sort of a second-hand shop selling garbage, basically. Didn't look like much at all, just plates, cutlery and shit. Then I saw this toolbox.

The drug deal telephone, Lighthouse Cinema, New York, 1996.
Photo: Silke Mayer

Well, you never know. So I opened it, and found it was filled with rolls of film. I could tell from the size of the reels that each film must have been about ten minutes long. Typical stag movie format. I bought the lot, about thirty in total. Only later did I discover what filthy little jewels I had picked up!"

An unkempt, unshaven gangster opened a door on the screen with a grin. It looked as if he was American, probably seeking refuge from native law enforcement agencies in Mexico. Black-haired girl #1 walked out, as black-haired girl #2 wandered in. Her dog was already waiting for her.

Mexican Dog was the title of the flick, and from the décor in it I'd say was made in the late 1920s. More than likely the film was used as the kinky climax to many a backroom screening night in the thirties and forties. "You must imagine," the guy next to me said excitedly, "the toolbox was probably original. In those days, you could go to jail for showing something like this. But people wanted to see it. Usually there would be a club of guys who found out about a supplier, who'd they then invite to the back room of a bar under some official-sounding guise..." He paused when the screen went blank, and dug around for a replacement. "Wait a minute, next movie... What about this one, from the 1910s? All human this time!"

After fumbling with the projector a little, the reel was loaded. A plush Parisian salon appeared on screen. The lonely lady in it was quick to receive visitors.

"Anyway," the scavenger embarked again on his story, "imagine how shows with this kind of material were back then. The guys would all be sitting there, smoking cigars and drinking whiskey; the barkeeper would admit only those people who could identify themselves with a certain sign or code word. Finally the guy in the repairman outfit arrived, the dirty movies hidden in his toolbox. Back then it was an adventure to see — and a bigger adventure to screen! — dirty movies..."

My attention drifted from the fucking threesome on the screen, down into the empty theatre. Was it an adventure to screen movies nowadays, I wondered? In a way it still was — at least in this place.

The Lighthouse cinema was Manhattan's only full-scale desolation row theatre. Its concrete slab ceiling in pieces barely supported the ugly neon lighting fixtures around the place; heaps of crumbling plaster painted green littered the base of each wall; mountains of old film prints were crammed beneath the screen; and — thanks to last night's punk rock concert there — the seats in the auditorium were now scattered all over.

The street bum who regularly showed up after a busy night, was downstairs noisily earning his living collecting bottles left over from the

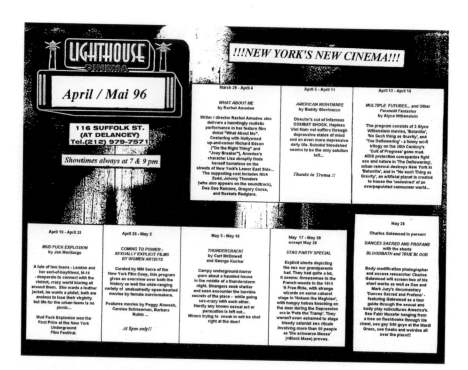

Programme schedule for April/May, 1996.

concert in a plastic bag. Every once in a while he stopped and glanced up at the activities on screen. Then he went on with his work.

"Your cinema is perfect for these movies," continued my guest with the red beard. "I don't want to sell them on like the other stuff I find; I think there is more money in showing them at a theatre — and it's certainly more fun. What about a fifty-fifty deal. I'll even get the movies announced on *The Howard Stern Show!*"

Maybe.

The setting was indeed perfect for these features. A foul playground for weird and dirty movies, where only the true connoisseur of the bizarre, daring, and absurd ever made a second visit; an underground trash nirvana in which I worked hard and all day for a return that hardly covered the cost of my bagels. Yet, I held onto the hope that the venue might strike a chord on the strings of downtown hipness. Where else could cinema-goers have such an absorbing experience, the movie playing being almost indistinguishable from the reality of the place? When *Thundercrack!* was screened a few days ago — an underground porn movie which takes place amidst a thunderstorm — a rainstorm outside the theatre came down so heavily that it infiltrated the five storey building to emerge from the ceiling right next to the screen. The expenditure for creating such a special effect would have been mind-boggling. I got it for free — thanks to a greedy slumlord and non-caring junkie neighbours.

Of course, I was lucky in that the storm outside didn't coincide with me screening a movie about thirsty settlers crossing a desert...

Gary Indiana had written in the *Village Voice* only the previous week: 'Do check out this little movie house, an extravagantly raw space in the middle of a senseless killing neighbourhood.'

Although I came to the theatre daily, I hadn't yet witnessed any killing in the area. But I liked the review — it sounded good. And anyway, I did once see a crowd chasing some guy who had tried to rob a grocery store, ready to lynch him. (They didn't catch him, though.)

Nor had my neighbour, whose heroin hiding place I destroyed when I moved in, yet complained. He must have thought his covert spot beneath a step on the stairway safe and secure, but alas hadn't reckoned on anyone wanting to construct a projection booth... I hammered away at the plaster under the staircase when a whole bunch of dime bags of heroin inscribed with the words 'Mortal Combat' fell into my hands. They made nice little gifts for the friends who had helped me with the place.

I fully appreciated that my neighbour would at some point discover his supply had disappeared, and I wasn't eager to be around when he did — similarly I knew that sooner or later the emissary of some other drug operation might show their face.

Hidden in a corner of the Lighthouse, I had found a telephone that had obviously been around since the place was a warehouse for a beauty shop. It still worked — only, whenever anyone called in, the phone would ring just once before relaying the caller to a piano store two blocks away. According to the locals, the piano store was a cover for a cocaine dealing operation. The call-forwarding attribute somehow obscured the source and the destination of the calls, a security measure should the police ever put a tap on the line. Even the bills were delivered to the theatre, listing reams of mysterious calls to Guatemala and Columbia, and quite a few I made myself to Europe. I threw the bills in the garbage. Free calls for me...

Another of the theatre's strange attractions happened to be pushing his bicycle into the auditorium. He took a seat at the sight of an ugly woman on screen inserting an eel into her cunt. It was Ian, the ratty bike messenger. My tenant. A skinny, pale Quasimodo figure, Ian actually lived here. He rented the tiny space at the back of the theatre for a few bucks a month.

"We've got to stop now," I told the smut peddler. "I have to clean the place up for the regular show at seven." Beer can in hand, my guest had sunken very comfortably into his seat. Reluctantly, he got up. "Neither one of us can lose if you give these pictures a run," he said. "I'm just asking for a percentage, not a guarantee."

"Thirty-five per cent for you and we've got a deal," I bartered, telling him, "That's still more than you'd get from any other Manhattan theatre — not that they would ever show these films, cowards that they are."

He mused over this offer as he packed away his toolbox. "Alright then, let's do it," he finally declared, and added optimistically, "There's always a crowd for this type of stuff."

I hoped so. What theatre manager didn't want a crowd? Not one night went by when I wasn't outside on the sidewalk, scanning the dreary street for a few more customers. They were easily distinguishable from the Hispanics who tended to populate the area: groups of young people or lonesome middle-aged cineasts, venturing off busy Delancey onto quiet Suffolk Street, eyeing each building with curiosity in their search for the barely visible cinema. The only give-away was a dimly lit store front window featuring the Lighthouse Cinema logo, and in a neon-lit box the title of the movie playing. Sort of a secret cinema, trying to remain below the radar of the fire marshal and the IRS, but at the same time still hoping to draw in the crowds.

High profile. Sign on the door of the Lighthouse. *Photo: Silke Mayer*

The Lighthouse had been written about in virtually every New York publication that had a section devoted to film or culture, from *New York Magazine* to porn-rag *Screw*, from *The New York Press* to the *Daily News*. The *New York Post* went so far as to call it 'New York's most unusual movie house,' whilst reviewing its schedule of films on a weekly basis and trying to hype the place as *the* new cult cinema. Only *Time Out* had the nerve to tell it straight: 'The Lighthouse may be the best-hyped but least attended movie house in town.'

The auditorium downstairs was a mess. The bum who was collecting the bottles had emptied the dregs straight onto the wooden floor — hadn't I told him a million times before to do that on the street? Beer was everywhere. I had to sweep it up, along with the cigarette butts and the bottles which the bum had missed while searching in the dark.

And there — oh, God! A huge chunk of plaster had fallen from the wall and almost destroyed a speaker. This place was far worse than any horror that might hit the screen. If one's attention drifted from, say, Joe Spinell slashing throats in *Maniac*, it might be drawn to the ceiling and the very real threat of being crushed by falling debris, or to the precarious floor where light from the basement shone between the rotten planks.

A thin wooden wall behind the screen separated the cinema from an abandoned beauty shop, in which homeless people squatted. Whenever there was a calm moment in the films that played, one could hear them yelling drunkenly at each other.

As I was sorting out the mess in the auditorium, I noticed a distinct lack of shouting and commotion from the other side of the panel wall. All I could hear was the barking of the homeless people's dog. But it was loud. The more I continued with my chore, the louder the dog became. It had started to work on the wall with alarming intensity. Was it trying to break through? The wall couldn't have been very stable, considering the burn-outs the landlord had employed to erect it...

I had to get a move on — it was already half-past-six. I shifted the seats back into their proper arrangement (in the direction of the screen), a job I was used to doing every Sunday. On Saturday nights, I held a party in the space, which helped to bring in a little extra cash. These comprised of DJs, beer, movies and live music — punk bands playing against a backdrop of old *Space Patrol* episodes, sci-fi, Popeye, Cold War propaganda, car accident footage, and sixties biker porn. It was the Lower East Side's roughest spot, but there was no doorman, no security, no fixed rules. Everything was permitted so long as the people who showed paid for their drinks. So far there had been no violence. Compared to the movie crowd, party thrill-seekers appeared to have a higher degree of tolerance for such a run-down joint — at least more of them showed up. Once, three-hundred people danced to a giant blow-job up on the screen.

The seats were done. On with the rest of the routine. I extinguished the neon lights, and illuminated instead the fairy lights strung along the walls. The place looked better already. Candles in wind-proof glass tubes, from a local Spanish grocery and decorated with bloody scenes of Christian martyrdom, where placed at my ticket desk and in the bathroom. The bathroom had hot water and even a shower, but no

electricity. So the candles served a practical purpose as well as an aesthetic one!

The bathroom was removed from the rest of the theatre, and to reach it patrons had to pass through bike messenger Ian's living room. I loved the faces people made when they opened the door expecting to find the bathroom, only to see instead a private space and a guy laying on the couch, smoking a joint and watching boxing on TV. "Bathroom is back there," or, "Bathroom is busy" is all that Ian would say.

Ian was sleeping, exhausted from whatever drug he had last ingested. I awoke him when I passed through his room, taking the candles to the bathroom. His face was dirty and partly covered with dried blood — nothing particularly unusual about that.

"Hi, Ian. How about the rent?" I asked. "You were paid on Friday didn't you?"

"I lost it," Ian replied.

"You lost it? How did that happen? Did you get mugged or something?"

Not only was Ian's face covered in dirt and blood, I now noticed that two of his front teeth were also missing. If I remembered correctly, he still had them yesterday.

"No, I just got drunk last night. Stinking drunk," said Ian with a new lisp. "I crashed my bicycle somewhere. And now my money is gone. Five-hundred bucks. I don't know where it went…"

It seemed as if I would have to wait another week for the rent. Or maybe two. I couldn't expect too much from a guy who was so down he had to live in a set-up like this — strangers walking through his living room at all hours, journalists at press screenings in the morning, party people late at night, and no window other than the one facing the devastated remains of the beauty shop (overlooking the squatters as they drank, fought and threatened him).

I cleaned the gates of the two 16mm projectors and threaded in the evening's feature: Buddy Giovinazzo's *American Nightmares*. A depressing gore movie, *American Nightmares* is the story of a Vietnam veteran who can't hack the daily grind after he returns home following internment in a Viet Cong torture camp. His wife hates him, his baby is an Agent Orange mutant, he is served with a notice of eviction, he has no money, and a gang of thugs is out to get him. Desperate, he spends his days wandering the streets trying without success to make some cash. Eventually he goes nuts.

Just as I almost did a few days ago.

My slumlord also owned the entire block, and the entire electricity supply for the block happened to pass through the cinema's meter. Whenever the electricity bill arrived in the mail, it was my task to simply hand it over to the landlord for settlement. But one time I got curious and opened the envelope… horrified to discover that $4,000

Projection booth at the Lighthouse. Photo: Silke Mayer

was long outstanding and a cut-off date threatened by the electricity company had already been and gone. As it was a Jewish holiday, I couldn't reach the slumlord. Neither did I have 4,000 bucks to prevent the blackout that seemed increasingly likely as time went on...

That very morning, a photographer arrived to work on a feature about the Lighthouse for *Paper Magazine*. While he nonchalantly spent hours preparing lights in the theatre for his photo shoot, I prayed with each moment that now wasn't the time the power would be suddenly cut off. In spite of it all, I managed a friendly grin for the camera! Whatever the immediate problem, I wanted to look optimistic in the magazine next month...

The same night, I had a relatively well publicised evening booked, for which the filmmaker MM Serra was set to appear in person. Could the show take place in candlelight without the power to run any films? Fortunately it never came to that as I managed to track down the landlord and got him to pay.

The first guests arrived for the screening of the notorious, uncut *American Nightmares*, including two fanzine editors, short on cash but generous with promise of how they would praise the cinema in their respective papers if I let them in for free. I let them in. More customers trickled through: a bunch of students, a couple of gore *otaku*, some friends of director Giovinazzo who were on the guest list. Ten paying customers in total. Not exactly great but the seventy bucks in my pocket was welcome, and I tried not to think too hard about paying the rent, and of the stack of bills I had at home. I started the projector, checked the focus and ran the film. I had seen *American Nightmares* many times before, so there was no reason for me to watch it again. Instead I set to work rewinding the party films of the previous night, my thoughts drifting off as I cranked the handle on the rewind table...

Six months ago, in the Fall of 1995, Dennis Nyback had closed his Pike Street Cinema in Seattle, a ragtag operation very similar to the one here. Convinced by his girlfriend to move to New York, he loaded the entire content of his theatre into a rental truck — projectors, screen, seats, curtains, his large film print collection, and an assortment of worthless garbage — and drove across the continent to New York.

On arrival, he called to ask if I wanted to run a cinema with him. I was pretty much the only film-related person he knew in town. Plus he knew I had experience, having already managed the Pike Street Cinema for him a couple of summers ago while he was out of town. It sounded like a wonderful opportunity. At the new theatre, Nyback assured me I would be able to screen all the wild and crazy stuff I always wanted to throw at an audience. And I did — or rather I did whenever I could afford the rental fees or knew how I could circumvent paying them. The latter option I achieved by getting private prints straight from directors, by ordering from print collectors instead of distributors, by locating cheaper foreign sources... I even went so far as to hand carry a heavy 35mm print all the way from the Berlin Film Festival just to save on transportation.

In December I found this space — the warehouse of Jaybra's Beauty Shop, which was in the process of going bankrupt. It was crammed with hundreds of boxes of shampoo, lining the shelves along the walls and piled up high on the floor. Over several cold and rainy mornings we packed the decrepit, forgotten bottles into a number of industrial-sized garbage containers. Most of the shampoo dated from the 1950s and carried legends that declared ominously:

West Point Hair Trainer
Smartly Disciplines Your Hair
Keeps Unruly Hair in Place
(No Affiliation With the West Point US Military Academy)

In amongst the above were Afro-Look stabilisers from the 1970s and other equally obscure, highly suspect looking lotions. I wore gloves for this particular clean-up job — something I hadn't done even when digging up bones as a gravedigger.

After removing the shampoo, some carpenter friends of mine installed a projection booth. And on we went with the shows — there simply wasn't the money for any further renovation. We emphasised the down-at-heel nature of the place, hoping that it would find its fans; people who could appreciate crudity and a freedom to smoke, drink, and eat take-out food while watching movies. Critics praised the space. A German filmmaker, Claudia Heuermann, announced that it was her favourite movie theatre in all of the world, and that she was preparing to make a documentary film about it.

She had recently arranged and shot here a gathering of jazz musicians like Anthony Coleman, Marc Ribot and Frank London for *Sabbath in Paradise* — a documentary about the Jewish avant-garde music scene.

Yet the general attendance remained low.

To create additional income, Dennis toured Europe's art houses with a couple of vintage animation film programs. On his return I would depart for a festival in Copenhagen to present a compilation of recent American underground movies.

Then, we would see.

I contemplated staying in Europe for a while to work — I'm an EC citizen and the wages are higher there. Revenue generated by the Lighthouse wasn't nearly enough to support the both of us at once...

I heard the door slam and jumped out of the projection booth. The black bum, a non-paying regular, was back. I had a bone to pick with him, and it didn't have anything to do with emptying beer over the floor (although that had pissed me off).

"Hey man," I said. "I let you in here for free many times, and I don't mind doing so. But your girlfriend — she always causes trouble. In ten minutes she will be here, yelling the whole place down looking for you to start a fight. Other people pay to come in and I have to protect them from bullshit like that."

"I'm a quiet man, you know that," the bum replied. "It's not my fault. She's a fuckin' crazy bitch. But what can you do? She's a girl and I ain't got no other one. I will tell her to keep out..."

"No, no, no. You've said that too may times now. Whenever you're here, it means trouble. Clear it up with her for good, stay quiet, and then you can both come back. It's the only way you're gonna see movies here again."

Friendly but persuasively, I led him out the door. Poor guy. He had been so happy to discover the cinema a few weeks ago. He told me that he hadn't seen a movie on a big screen for years, and that he used to love to see them that way. However, I couldn't have my customers being harassed night after night, simply because I felt compassion for a movie-loving bum.

Ha! The blood-soaked finale had hit the screen. It was the part of *American Nightmares* that invariably drew my attention back to the film and which I could watch without tiring over and over again: Ricky, the Vietnam vet, had been out wandering the streets all day. The answer to his problems had dawned on him — he had to kill himself. Ricky returns home and puts a gun to his head. Before firing off a shot however, he lowers the revolver and methodically walks over to the living room. "I love you, Cathy," he says to his wife. She turns around to face the barrel of his gun. Ricky empties bullets into her. "Die! Die!" he demands as she lies on the floor, blood spurting from her mouth. "Die!" Ricky fires again, finally killing her. He then turns his attention to the crying mutant baby. One bullet is enough to tear it to pieces.

Ricky returns to the kitchen. His own death — the inextricable conclusion — draws painfully closer. But Ricky is thirsty. The faucet is dead. He opens the fridge, removes from it the milk that was already sour and undrinkable at the beginning of the film, and pours the lumpy

The bloody finale of *American Nightmares* aka *Combat Shock*. *Photo courtesy: Buddy Giovinazzo*

Previous page: The Lighthouse auditorium (with nasty neon lights). *Photo: Silke Mayer*

mess down his throat. At that moment the faucet begins to drip. Too late. He uses the remaining bullet to splash his brains against the wall. The end.

"Great movie!"

"Enjoyed it a lot!"

"Hey, I haven't seen such a relentless massacre on screen in ages!"

These were some of the comments customers made as they were leaving the theatre. I was at the door chatting with them, convincing them that many similarly worthwhile movies were coming up, and pushing into their hands schedules for future programmes. A few said they liked the place, and would return with their friends. Time would tell.

Five people for the following nine o'clock show. Not too bad a night. It brought in a hundred bucks — enough for me to get by on for the time being.

For the next week, I had booked Alyce Wittenstein's *Multiple Futures... And Other Paranoid Fantasies*. It was to be the New York premiere of a movie trilogy by a local cult filmmaker. Wittenstein was scheduled to attend in person. That should bring in a few people. Ever the optimist, I looked to the greener pastures that lay ahead...

Right now it was time for me to leave. I would buy a forty ounce bottle of Budweiser, take it home and continue writing the programme notes for the short movies I planned to take on a tour of Japan later in the fall. I would finish the evening on the phone to my Japanese girlfriend in far away San Mateo, California.

Before I closed the shutter on the Lighthouse, it was necessary to wake Ian. He had to lock the building from within. At my insistence he rose dreamily from his nap. "Just give me a few minutes. I will lock it later," he said in his half-daze. I knew Ian too well. "You will fall asleep the moment I'm gone," I warned him. "If you don't come now, I'll lock it from the outside."

That got him up. One time I had locked the shutter from the outside, not realising Ian was still in the building. It left him trapped and — not having my home phone number — unable to reach me. He eventually managed to get free by ordering Chinese take-out food, and slipping the key beneath the shutter to the delivery guy.

On my way home, down dimly lit Essex Street, I passed the black bum and his girlfriend as they were scavenging the garbage bags outside Clayton's Gallery.

"The movie man!" she yelled from across the street.

"We love you!" chirped the bum.

Fuck you.

The Lighthouse Cinema on 116 Suffolk Street existed from February through September 1996.

East of Siberia
Scenes from the
North Korean Film Front

Bizarre movies have always held a strong fascination for me, so too the places where such movies come from. Having spent years living in the bowels of the Lower East Side and arranging screenings for the rabid assaults of the New York Cinema of Transgression, and after devoting myself to the seedier sides of Tokyo and the works of the Japanese "Cyberpunk" radicals,* North Korea felt like an obvious place to go next. A hostile half of a partitioned peninsula, it was governed like the compound of a messianic sect by a movie-mad, booze-swilling semi-god leader, and producing movies with titles like *The Sea of Blood*, *Woman Warrior of Koryo* and *The Women Volunteers* — what else could I wish for?

But one cannot simply go and buy a ticket to travel there; North Korea is one of the most isolated countries in the world and will allow in very few visitors.

Luck was on my side, however. At the Berlin Film Festival in February 1999, I mentioned my pipe dream about visiting North Korea to a friend who ran an independent cinema in Berlin. To my surprise he replied: "You want to meet North Korean film people? Some North Koreans come to our office a couple of times every week, who we help in getting Western films for screenings at their embassy — or whatever else they do with them. Nobody knows for sure what they're up to."

*I toured Japan with a programme of American underground films in 1997 (which included a screening at a Shinto Shrine in Fukuoka), showed a programme of uncensored vintage US porn in various Japanese cities in 1999, and did intensive research on the Japanese underground film scene. All this and more will be revealed in a future book!

As it turned out, the visitor to which my friend referred was the Secretary for Economic Affairs of the "Office for the Protection of the Interests of the Democratic People's Republic of Korea in Berlin" — the diplomatic bureau that North Korea maintains in Germany. He would meet regularly with the cinema organisers, presenting them with a fresh list of film titles on each occasion. He never knew what the movies were about, nor who had made them or any other details, but it was always very urgent business. "Get us 35mm prints of the films," he would say. "Money isn't important, and it doesn't matter what language the films are in. We want to show them in our embassy."

Without fail the prints would be returned after two weeks, and the rental fee would be settled expediently and without fuss. Were the films really for screening at the embassy? It was anyone's guess. But considering how the Great Leader back home was an ardent movie buff, and that the primary concern for the Secretary for Economic Affairs appeared to be locating pics like *Air Wolf* and Jackie Chan's *Police Story 1* and *2*, there had to be more to it than that. Berlin is a city in which it is very easy to find film prints of all kinds. Perhaps the North Koreans were using the embassy as a front to get prints for the private film screenings of the Great Leader, Kim Il-sung?

Only days after returning home to Nuremberg, I got a call from the cinema in Berlin. "We told the North Koreans about your plans," my friend relayed to me down the line. "They have some high-ranking official here in Berlin right now. He wants to see you. Get here as quickly as possible."

I did. The North Korean officials were Mr Paek, Vice President of the Korea Film Export and Import Corporation, and his translator Mr Kim. Accompanying them was Mr U, the mysterious regular visitor to the cinema and hirer of films. It was a rather formal meeting. The North Koreans looked completely out of place in the sleek high-tech surrounds of the cinema office, wearing cheap ill-fitting suits and badges on their lapels that featured a picture of Kim Il-sung.

I told them about a recent tour I had made of European cinemas with a package of fourteen Japanese movies, and that my intention was hopefully to do likewise with a package of North Korean movies. But first, of course, I had to view some North Korean films to make a selection — and I had to visit North Korea. I couldn't possibly introduce a programme of films to European audiences without having first been to the country of their origin. How would I answer questions from the press? How could I write programme notes on the films without a first-hand knowledge of their background and the society from which they emerged?

Finally, after much debating and many cups of coffee, the ambassadors for North Korea arrived at a decision. "Well," announced Mr Paek, "our international film festival takes place only once in every two years.

This year, it doesn't take place. But we can invite you to the Korea Film Show in September in Pyongyang. There, you can make your selection."

Reception committee for the marathon girl at Pyongyang airport, 1999.
Photo: J Schönherr

Part 1

Come September 4, 1999, I was seated on an Air Koryo plane, having travelled from Beijing and now touching down on the landing strip of Pyongyang Airport. My initial glimpse from the air had confirmed what I'd already heard about the scarcity and poverty of North Korea. I saw a long stretch of empty motorway — one stationary car in the whole of the four lanes as far as the eye could see. On the country roads was the occasional bicycle, but by and large everyone travelled on foot. Oxen were employed to work the arable land.

In front of the airport, however — easily identifiable by the large portrait of Kim Il-sung on top — a great scene was unfolding: several hundred people in uniform were lined up, carrying red flags and banners bearing slogans in Korean. It was a meticulously organised reception committee comprising of saluting soldiers, women in traditional dress and children with red scarves around their necks. I hoped this wasn't for the Korea Film Show. It was a little overboard and far too much for a first-time visitor. But word had spread quickly among the UN aid workers and diplomats crowding the plane that a North Korean marathon runner, winner of a gold medal in some competition, was on board the flight. This reception was for her. While the passengers tried to snap some photos from the plane's windows, North Korean army news men in uniform, carrying vintage 16mm cameras, ran frantically around on the tarmac. We couldn't really see the marathon

The Korea Film Show Pyongyang, Sept 1999

runner once she had left the plane — only the ebbing throng of camera-men and welcoming officials swarming around her.

Eventually, the crowd began to disperse and we were allowed off the plane — transported by bus the 150 meters to the airport building. Everything appeared in order with my papers. The immigration officer made no remark about the South Korean stamps in my passport — souvenirs of an earlier trip — nor my visa, which I had obtained only the day before in Beijing. I entered a hallway where passenger luggage was laid out on the concrete floor. Before I could find my bag, I was approached by a short-haired woman in her forties. "You must be Johannes Schönherr from Germany," she said. "I'm your guide for your time in Korea. Welcome!" She must have studied my photo well — but

At Kim Il-sung's 'birthplace' at Mangyongdae. (From left to right) Miss Choe, Mr Paek, the author, a local guide, and Mr Sok.

then again, I was probably the only male in the country with long hair.

Customs procedures were surprisingly straight forward. The only thing the authorities seemed concerned about were cellular phones. This was the only reason they x-rayed the luggage. Nobody chose to look at the books in my bag.

Once through the check, my guide — Miss Choe of the Korea Film Export and Import Corporation — led me to a red bus. "Are there many people coming for the Korea Film Show?" I inquired. "No, only one more," she replied. "A young man from Switzerland."

The young man from Switzerland finally arrived. His many bags had netted him a more thorough search at customs. "Hi, I'm Nicolas Righetti from Geneva," he said as he peered in through the door of the bus. Miss Choe announced that we were in a hurry and that he should get on board quickly. Driving towards the city, I noticed that the commuters outside appeared to all be moving together as one, in one long line, like a giant millipede. I chatted with Nicolas, curious about the only other foreigner invited to attend the event to which we were headed. He had no idea what the Korea Film Show was about, but shared my belief that it must be some kind of national showcase.

The bus was stopped at a checkpoint, as was every other vehicle entering the city of Pyongyang. The driver yelled something in Korean to the guard and pointed towards us, the foreigners. The guard waved the bus through immediately.

The first concrete slab buildings of Pyongyang came into sight. Even more people lined the street, walking towards the city.

Suddenly, the tired-looking Miss Choe turned and asked me: "Mr Schönherr, don't you feel especially honoured that this festival is taking place only for you?"

"Huh? What do you mean?" I replied, a little shocked.

"You wanted the chance to see some of our movies here," she continued. "Well, the Korea Film Show gives you this opportunity."

"No, I know nothing about that," I said. "I thought the Korea Film Show was some kind of festival and I'm its guest. I never knew anything about a festival just staged for me... "

My head was trying to assimilate this information, what it meant, and the possible ramifications of being in a strange country that thinks my visit important enough that it has to create and organise a whole event.

"What about Mr Righetti?" I asked. "He was invited, too."

"I don't know about him. He has his own guide," said Miss Choe, in a manner that sounded more like a sigh than a statement. "You can ask Mr Sok."

Mr Sok was the chain-smoking official sitting next to the driver, who wore sunglasses and carried a rather camp little leather handbag. We had met briefly at the airport, but he had otherwise remained perfectly quiet. Nicolas seemed to know him, however.

"I'm the Chief of Operations in Western Europe for the Korea Film Export and Import Corporation," Mr Sok introduced himself. "But despite being in this position and going to Paris a few times," he continued with a hint of resignation, "it was Mr Paek who discovered you. He is the bigger official and has much bigger eyes than I do."

"But you invited Mr Righetti?" I asked, not so much a question as it

The Pyongyang Hotel.
Photo: J Schönherr

Farm produce outlet on a
Pyongyang street corner.
Photo: Christian Karl

was an attempt to lift Mr Sok's spirit.

"Yes," Mr Sok announced with pride, smiling broadly. "He is a good friend of ours. He is now here on his third visit."

We stuck to side streets that ran parallel with the main street through the city. At every junction I could see the reason for our detour: masses of people were lined up along the main thoroughfare. "What's happening?" I asked.

"Our heroine Jong Song-ok was awarded the gold medal for her victory in the world marathon competition in Seville, Spain," replied Miss Choe. "Now our people are welcoming her."

"I was in the plane with her," stated Nicolas. "From Stuttgart to Beijing she was sitting only a few seats away, and she seemed *so* tired."

This close encounter with the national heroine didn't raise any eyebrows on the bus.

"We arrive soon," Miss Choe advised. "Please stay in your hotel rooms. We will have a meeting soon."

The bus turned into the parking lot of the Pyongyang Hotel. "Sorry we cannot accommodate you better this time," apologised Miss Chloe. "Mr Nicolas, on your other visits you have stayed in some of the better hotels we have here. But this time, we don't have that much of a budget."

The hotel room was fine with me. Much better than the cheap and battered hotel I had stayed at during my few nights in Beijing. I turned on the TV: pictures of Pyongyang streets lined with thousands of people awaiting the marathon girl. Looking out of my window, I could see that her route took her right by the hotel. Should I stay inside and watch her home-coming reception on TV as I had been told? Or...?

I had read that in North Korea visitors are not expected to walk the streets alone — only with the accompaniment of a guide. The decision was made for me when I ran into Nicolas on the stairway.

"You wanna come with me?" he grinned. "It's no problem. We just go out. I've done it many times before. But be quiet."

We headed out, along the street on which the many thousands were lined. With Nicolas carrying a big video camera on his shoulder, we must have looked like a Western TV crew. Children waved their little red flags at us, laughed and seemed to be having a good time. But whenever the children got too excited about our foreign faces, a teacher would always put them back in their place. It wasn't long before we caught the attention of North Korean camera crews, who decided to follow our every move, no doubt under the assumption that we were an important Western TV team covering their country's great victory.

"Isn't it crazy? I love this place!" Nicolas kept shouting. "There's no place on the fucking planet like it!"

The marathon girl came down the street, standing upright in a speeding Mercedes cabriolet. I got just a brief glimpse of her. She seemed worn out and stood in the car like a statue, clutching lots of flowers. Everyone cheered.

A minute later the event was over. People began to disperse, as policewomen blew their whistles like crazy at anyone who attempted to cross the street short of using the designated underpasses at the intersections.

Suddenly, we were approached by Mr Kim — the same Mr Kim who I'd met in Berlin, and who was now Nicolas' guide.

"Where have you been?" he asked. "You know we have a meeting now. I have been searching for you." "Uh, we were just looking at your people celebrating," Nicolas responded, which seemed to be excuse enough for the time being. We hurried back to the hotel, sticking to the crowded, dimly lit underpasses at each crossroads — as necessitated by North Korean traffic law.

At the hotel we met Mr Paek, Mr Sok and Miss Choe, who were

seated in one of the corners of the hallway. Mr Paek was as stiff and as solemn as he was at the Berlin meeting. He handed each of us a type-written itinerary of the days to come. Lots of visits to monuments and lots of films to see. We seemed to have no time of our own. Okay, we came here to see films but...? "It's a free country, do what you please in your free time," Mr Paek said, making no remark about our having just disappeared from our supposedly ever watchful guides... "Now, please, have a rest in your rooms," Mr Paek concluded. "We will meet in the morning."

We agreed to everything he said, but our actual plans were different. We wanted to head out again — alone. It was almost evening now; a shower, some hotel food and we would be gone.

Except it didn't work out that way.

Miss Choe met us at our rooms and led us to the hotel restaurant. "Sorry, it's not open yet," she apologised, and seated herself next to Mr Sok at the entrance to the restaurant. I was looking for some topic of conversation, and remembered what a Japanese film critic had once told me: North Korea had a much wider variety to offer in terms of traditional Korean dog-meat dishes than did the South. Miss Choe seemed perplexed. "You really think Korean people eat dogs?" she said in response to my line of conversation. "Who told you that?"

"Well, it's kind of common knowledge in the West," I said. "I was actually told by a Japanese film festival visitor who came here a few years ago."

"Who was that?"

"Um, sorry — I forgot the name. Is that information wrong?"

"This person is a liar!" said Miss Choe, a little upset. "We don't eat dogs!"

Feeling somewhat sorry for having pursued that particular topic of conversation (and the fact I was unlikely to experience the delicacy of dog meat in North Korea, just as I had failed to do so far in the South), I walked over to a big display on the wall featuring a rocket.

"What's this?" I asked, trying to make the question sound as innocuous as possible.

"This is the satellite we shot into orbit," Miss Choe replied dutifully, "although the Japanese imperialists claim it is a war rocket. They try to hurt our country with their war-mongering propaganda..."

"What was the satellite for?" I inquired further. The reply was simply "Umm..."

I proposed that it might have been for scientific purposes, although to me it just looked like a regular military rocket.

"Oh, yes," said Miss Choe. "Scientific purposes."

The doors to the restaurant eventually swung opened, relieving Miss Choe of any more uncomfortable questions. "You have table eighteen," she said as she waved Nicolas and myself through. "Good night."

The food was vaguely Western and not very good. A middle-aged European couple who looked non-too happy, sat at the table next to us. We quickly fell into conversation with them. He was a basketball trainer from Yugoslavia, he said, unable to find a job in his home country because of recent political upheavals and resulting economic troubles. He explained that at an international championship, the North Koreans had approached him and offered him good money if he would live and train one of their teams here for a year. He made the deal. Together with his wife he had been living in the Pyongyang Hotel for only six weeks, and both were already looking forward to the end of the contract.

"How good is the pay?" I asked.

"It's good," he replied, "but when the year is over, we will have to spend it all on a psychiatrist. And maybe on our divorce." They laughed.

Each had their own guide watching over them. Of course, sometimes they would manage to sneak away and breathe some fresh air alone — but that was rare.

A short but stocky man who was drunk came to our table. "*U menya Sasha*," he introduced himself, babbling away in Russian, not caring whether we understood him or not. From what we could grasp, he was also a basketball trainer, but — unlike the Yugoslavs — had lived here for quite a while. His main interest was drinking *sul*, Korean hard liquor. He invited us up to his room and asked that we bring some sul. The Yugoslavians had made a quick exit when they saw him coming, and it took us quite a while and the promise that we would join him later before we were able to shake free of him.

Living in North Korea for any considerable amount of time didn't seem particularly healthy for the brain...

Well, what now? Drinking, for sure, but not with the Russian guy.

"The last two times I came here, everything was easy," Nicolas said. "Don't worry. Let's just go out and grab a beer. We don't need a guide."

We made it as far as the hotel lounge before being intercepted by Mr Kim.

"Where are you going?" he asked.

"Going out to get a beer. Don't worry."

"But you don't know Pyongyang."

"Well, I found bars in the strangest corners of Albania," Nicolas replied. "I'm sure I'll find one in the capital of the Democratic People's Republic of Korea."

Seeing that he couldn't stop us, Mr Kim simply joined us.

We walked with him through the same street that the big reception had been staged earlier in the day. Without illumination from street lights and with only the occasional apartment window glowing dimly, it was now pitch dark. Every room into which we managed to catch a glimpse we saw portraits of the two Great Leaders hanging on the wall:

Kim Il-sung, the father and original Great Leader, and his son Kim Jong-il, who'd taken over after his father died in 1994. Starting out as the Dear Leader, Kim Jong-il had since made it to the exalted status of Great Leader. His father, however, remained president for all eternity — people continued to pray for him in heaven or wherever a Great Leader resides after shedding his mortal coil.

Very few people and fewer cars were on the street. The occasional, always overcrowded Czech Tatra tramway zoomed by ghostlike. Pyongyang didn't seem to have an abundance of bars. It took us a while to reach a barbecue restaurant near Kim Il Sung Square, which was almost a hangout for the locals — but not quite. The bar served Chinese Yanjing beer and took *blue won* — foreigner money. It didn't particularly look it, but the place was apparently upscale.

North Korea has several kinds of money. *Blue won* is given in exchange for Western currency and can only be spent at designated places; *brown won* is for the general population. A foreigner can't get brown won and thus can't buy anything from places not licensed to deal with foreigners.

Nicolas and Mr Kim reminisced about days gone by. Nicolas, it turned out, had come to North Korea for the first time in 1998, when he attended the Pyongyang Film Festival to show some of his documentaries. As head of the Swiss delegation, he was invited back to the annual April Culture Festival in 1999 — where his delegation won the main prize or gold medal or something. To his astonishment, a few weeks ago he received a letter from Mr Sok inviting him back, this time to attend the "Korea Film Show".

About that particular event we would find out more in the morning.

First things first, however. The morning was set aside for the one official function every visitor to North Korea must respect: placing flowers in front of the statue of Kim Il-sung at the top of Mansudae Hill, a structure as high as a skyscraper that overlooked the city. It was a rather chilly morning, quite suited for such a solemn ceremony.

The Kim Il-sung statue on Mansudae Hill. *Photo: Christian Karl*

But it wasn't that ceremonial in the end — Mr Paek simply gave me a bunch of flowers, which I plonked down on top of a pile of other flowers all wrapped in plastic. Our guides then took photos to commemorate the "event".

From Mansudae Hill we overlooked the bizarre concrete structures of various sports stadiums, revolutionary monuments of all shapes and sizes, and an endless mass of Eastern European-style housing projects. From the bus on the way down, we also had a clear view of the Ryongyong Hotel — or rather, of its incomplete construction. The 105 storey pyramid of the Ryongyong Hotel absolutely dominates the skyline of Pyongyang. Knowing about it already, I decided to bait Miss

Choe: "What is that big pyramid?"

At that moment the bus took a turn and the building was obscured from view by trees. "What pyramid?" Miss Choe replied, "I can't see a pyramid."

At its inception, the Ryongyong was meant to be the "tallest hotel in Korea". Construction on it commenced — so legend has it — when Kim Jong-il heard that a South Korean company was building a 103 storey hotel in Singapore. He wanted his part of Korea to have an even higher one, especially when considering it could have been host to guests of the 1988 Olympics. Alas, the Olympics ended up as a purely South Korean affair with no Northern involvement at all. North Korea had boycotted the games, and in so doing lost the spirit to finish the pyramid hotel. They continued half-heartedly on its construction until 1991, after which time it was patently obvious that Pyongyang would never

The shell that is the Ryongyong Hotel.
Photo: Christian Karl

see completion of the 300-metre tall pyramid with its seven revolving restaurants. There was no money with which to finish it, and not enough expertise on how best to continue. What remained was this great empty shell — of which postcards are available. They show what appears to be a magnificent, occupied building at sunset with light shining brightly from within. Looking closely one can tell that the last rays of the sun are shining through the empty window frames of a white elephant...

The "Korea Film Show" could start. Held in the screening room of the Film Export and Import Corporation, it was indeed a series of screenings held solely for Nicolas and myself. There were no film directors or publicity people to meet, and no audience outside of us two —

with the exception that Mr Paek and Mr Sok would occasionally sit in on the screenings with us. Almost none of the films had subtitles, but the room did have a microphone and speaker system through which Miss Choe or Mr Kim could translate the dialogue into English.

The very first film was a relatively recent production called *A Far-Off Islet*. It told the story of a young teacher living on an isolated island, whose school has only two kids. Her desire is to relocate to Pyongyang because "she wants to be close to the Great Leader Kim Jong-il". Events transpire that enlighten her to the fact that her true place is indeed on the island. In the end the Great Leader sends her his regards, praising her as "a heroine of our time".

I liked the dramatic scene where the teacher is pedalling her bicycle to produce power from her bicycle dynamo for the beacon of the local lighthouse, thus saving a ship from crashing into the cliffs. But otherwise *A Far-Off Islet* was rather tedious.

The first North Korean film of my life was a disappointment. Over the course of the next few of days, I would explain to Mr Paek that I wanted to see films packed with action, evil Americans, Southern spies, real drama and contemporary conflicts. And I wanted to see *Pulgasari,* the North Korean Godzilla movie I had heard so much about in Japan, where it played theatrically in 1998 and did well.

Mr Paek did understand my requests for "strong movies" and he made a great effort to get me films that would meet my demands. With Nicolas, it was a little more difficult. He had never been a film show organiser, let alone a distributor, but that, it seemed, was how Mr Sok had regarded Nicolas when he invited him. Nicolas just said: "Show me some documentaries — that's more my field." He was a documentary filmmaker, not a film sales person.

The next two days at the screening room brought a marked improvement in Mr Paek's selection of films. We got to see hilarious Korean War taekwondo spoofs, cute war heroines, and medieval swordfighters. One film even featured the lazy son of a North Korean labour hero, who has doubts about the arduous nature of North Korean progress. Of course in the end, he learns to find his place in society and becomes a labour hero himself. My favourite movie however was *My Happiness*, starring two cute girls drafted into the North Korean army during the Korean War (1950–53). One scene had the chief nurse of the girlie unit swimming over to a South Korean warship, whipping hand grenades out from beneath her jacket and screaming, "Long live Kim Il-sung!" before blowing the ship and herself to bits. In another scene, the missing boyfriend of one of the main heroines returns home after the war. To everyone's amazement his legs are intact. Rumour had it that he'd lost them both, but it transpires that emergency doctors in

Apartment buildings in downtown Pyongyang.

Next Page: Arc of Triumph, celebrating victory over the Japanese.
Photos: J Schönherr

the field saved them by transplanting their own bones and muscles!

Topping *My Happiness* however, was *Forever in Our Memory*, a brand new 1999 picture. It dealt with the terrible weather calamities and resulting food shortages of recent years — using cinema to try and turn disaster into propagandist nonsense. Regimental commander Ri Chol-suk receives orders to take his platoon into the starvation zone and help folk in the countryside battle against the bad weather. This they achieve by carrying buckets of water for miles to overcome drought, and using their own bodies to build a dam and hold back flood waters!

Propaganda doesn't get much more audacious than this! What a display of utterly unbelievable heroism! That said, however, the Great Leader is without question always the biggest hero — in spite of the fact that he is never overtly pictured or portrayed in any feature film. Here, his presence is denoted by the tire tracks he leaves in the dust, over which the people of the countryside clamour with true religious fervour.

My misgivings at not being allowed to move around without a guide were easing off. I looked at it stoically: outwardly comply to all that is asked of you while, in reality, secretly do whatever you want anyway. It was the same as in any dictatorship. I had a lot of fun educating Miss Choe on life in Western Europe, while both Nicolas and myself found ways of getting around town unattended.

It was great to be on the streets, free to explore. We saw girls in "Shock Brigade" uniforms marching tirelessly in step, determined young men with red flags over their shoulders, and war veterans laden with medals hobbling in and out of the subway — it was like being in our own personal weird Communist propaganda movie, just like the ones we'd been watching these past few days! Given the fact that every second person was in uniform, nobody in the street seemed to care that here we were, foreigners, walking around without the all-important omnipresent guide.

There was one exception: I hadn't been in the train station for long when I was thrown out by a female officer. Not that there was particularly much to see, anyway, unlike the parks surrounding the station where people from the countryside hung around waiting for their train.

They were evidently a lot poorer than the Pyongyang city dwellers. Still, it was a far cry from the famine said to be plaguing North Korea, as reported by the media in the West. The propaganda machine here did admit to some problems — as depicted in *Forever in Our Memory* — but there was no evidence of anyone actually starving to death... at least not in the capital.

One night, the whole city had a power failure that lasted several hours. Nicolas and I were sitting in the hotel restaurant when it happened. Through the window we could see that the city was in complete darkness, except for the Juche tower, which still had all its lights on. We decided go over.

The tower was located in a park on the Taedong River, the huge "flame" on top — a twenty-metre high electrical torch — burning all the more brighter in the pitch black night. According to a documentary film I had seen, the tower symbolised "the greatness of the immortal Juche idea, bringing its incredible light to the world for all to see". There weren't many people around, and certainly no evidence of the bored teenagers who would congregate at such a place were it in the West. The few shadowy figures gave one another a wide berth, and all had their nose buried deep in a book. Party manifestos that carried more clout when read under the influence of the tower's shining beacon, perhaps? No — I was later told

The Tower of the Juche Idea, and (below) the commemorative plaques inside it, which show that the Great Leader is loved all over the world. *Photos: J Schönherr*

these people were desperate for a light whatever the source, frantically cramming for an exam the following day...

Juche is the central ideology or "religion" of the country, governing every aspect of daily life. In short, Juche transforms the Great Leaders into virtual gods and asserts that North Korea must deal with all of its issues and problems with absolute independence — just like every other country should. The latter idea finds its expression in often-repeated slogans like "Kim Jong-il is leading the whole world to independence!" Of late, right-wing activists in Europe have found a certain affinity in Juche: fuck capitalism, kick the foreigners out and keep the nation pure.

I would have preferred to stay in Pyongyang — watching movies most of the day and hanging around the city unguarded — but the visitor's schedule didn't allow it. I had to go to Mount Myohyang on an overnight trip. Nicolas had been there before and, with a little persuasion, he was able to talk our hosts out of having to go a second time. I had no such excuse. Mr Sok, Miss Choe, along with the driver who had brought us from the airport on our arrival, still attired in his cool black uniform, accompanied me to Mount Myohyang.

The trip took two hours, on a four-lane motorway almost void of any other vehicles. We did pass the occasional truck by the roadside, however, where drivers tried to repair an engine surrounded by a diligent group of people all awaiting their ride to resume.

I had a good time talking to Miss Choe. I discovered she had been to other countries, such as China, Bangladesh, and Thailand. But the experiences she drew from travelling abroad differed greatly to mine. For her, Beijing was simply confusing — too many people, too many cars, too much chaos. She wasn't used to such pandemonium and it scared her. To me, Beijing was great — a city in the full swing of development. But I could understand Miss Choe's apprehension; her background was very different to mine, and even different to that of the Chinese. In a way she reminded me of a typical "Protestant mother" — always helpful, always open to other opinions, but staunchly unswerving when it came to her own religion (which was Juche).

But this wasn't an issue right now, and we were happy to talk about life in various places outside of North Korea.

The Hyangsan Hotel was a huge structure built by a Japanese company, but apart from myself and a Taiwanese tourist group of about thirty people, it stood pretty much empty. The information brochure boasted of two cinemas being inside, so I inquired at the reception desk as to what was playing.

"Well... nothing," came the reply.

Miss Choe told me that she and Mr Sok would be served much humbler meals than myself at dinner time, and so left me to dine and spend the night alone. What to do in this empty hotel complex? Unfortunately, wandering around outside wasn't an option — as the hotel was situated in the middle of a dark forest there would be nothing to see there.

After writing a few postcards, I went down to the lobby where a small Korean group watched a re-run of the marathon girl's victory in Seville on TV. The hotel bar wasn't open anymore, but I discovered a small karaoke bar, where three drunk Taiwanese men were singing along to a tape they had evidently brought along themselves. Staying there wasn't really an option, so I bought some bottled beer to take to my room. Schlitz from Milwaukee was the only thing available, about the worst American beer on sale in the world.

I settled down in front of the TV to find that the last programme on the only channel had just finished.* The radio also had only one station to offer, featuring a "revolutionary" mix of traditional Korean and Western musical elements, and pretty much the last thing I wanted to hear. There wasn't much else left other than to turn in early and go to sleep — as all North Koreans do, according to Miss Choe.

In the morning, we went to the International Friendship Exhibition — the sole reason for us coming to the Hyangsan hotel and the only reason the motorway had been built into the mountains in the first place. The exhibition complex consisted of two buildings: one housed diplomatic gifts to Kim Il-sung and the other, smaller one, gifts to Kim Jong-il. The construct went deep into the mountain. There were no windows, only doors weighing several tons, and tunnels that went much deeper than we were allowed to see. The exhibition complex supposedly doubled as a nuclear shelter for the government.

No effort was spared to erect the exterior buildings. Shaped like traditional Korean wooden structures, they were made entirely of marble and granite. We had to wear slippers while walking through them, so not to damage the precious floors. The exhibitions themselves were hilarious. Not so much Kim Jong-il's exhibition — there wasn't much in that one to see — but Kim Il-sung's. I often wondered what an internationally recognised dictator might receive as gifts — well, here was the answer. The items on display ranged from the pathetic, to the super-kitsch, to the expensive. There was a fruit bowl from Jimmy Carter, presented when he brokered the nuclear arms deal in 1994 (and which looked like it had been filched from a Soho coffee-house dishwasher); porcelain doves awarded by American religious leader Billy Graham

*North Korea has only one regular channel. Only on holidays does there operate a second and third TV channel. Of course, no foreign channel is available.

(there were several porcelain doves on display; apparently Graham travelled to North Korea quite often... well, if he ever wound up running a state it probably wouldn't be that much different to North Korea); a bear skin from Romanian dictator Nicolae Ceaucescu; a hunting rifle from East German head-of-state Erich Honecker; a set of petroleum lamps given by Emperor Bokassa of Central Africa (who was later imprisoned for cannibalism)... I forget what the gift from Pol Pot of Cambodia had been, because we were hurrying by the glass display cabinets so quickly. Mr Sok skipped the tour. I was accompanied only by Miss Choe, and a local guide — a young girl who spoke only Korean.

We made a special stop at the German display. Here the guide knew little about the individual pieces, and so I became an impromptu guide. There was a little piece of the Berlin Wall, awarded by writer Luise Rinser; a Ernst Thälmann bronze statue* was a gift from the DKP, the

Mt. Myohyang 妙香山(ミョヒヤン山)

조선 · 평양 Pyongyang · Korea

West German Communist party financed by the East Germans that never got higher than two per cent in any election (two percent being a generous figure); a Thälmann plaque was the gift presented by the West German KPD, a leftist splinter group of the seventies...

Miss Choe dutifully translated all my remarks to the local guide, though they were sometimes taken aback by what I said: *"What? The Communists getting only two per cent in elections?"*

We came eventually to a set of wine glasses, another gift from Ceaucescu. I told the story I was itching to tell. "You know," I said. "Ceaucescu owned a collection of state gifts similar to those in this exhibition before he was shot in 1989. The collection was auctioned off just last month. People from all over the world came to bid for some of the tackiest stuff."

Neither Miss Choe nor the guide had heard that Ceaucescu had been

*Thälmann being the leader of the German Communist party in the 1930s. He ran against Hitler in the 1933 election.

executed by his own military.

The less-than-exciting road trip back to Pyongyang was again made pleasant with conversation and laughter. Miss Choe accompanied me into the hotel restaurant, where Nicolas was already seated at a table. She left to talk to some other people, and I immediately launched into how much of a cool and fun time I had up on Mount Myohyang. He stopped me cold. "I didn't have such a good time here," he said. "Mr Kim accused me of being a spy and later tonight I have to have a talk with Mr Sok about it." Nicolas looked pale and drawn. "You know what it means here to be accused of spying?"

"Don't worry," I responded with undue optimism. "I can help you."

I yelled over to Miss Choe. "Please come here, there's a small problem that needs fixing."

Miss Choe came over, ever ready to help out, but a little curious at the same time. "Our friend here has been accused of being a spy," I said. "Do you have any advice on what to do?"

"No," she replied without a moment's hesitation and left as quickly as should she could.

Not a good sign.

"What happened?" I asked.

"I've got a lot of camera equipment with me and they don't like that at all," Nicolas explained. "And I went out a lot. Sometimes at five in the morning, getting lots of great shots around the city."

This was true; I knew a bit about it. Indeed I was no angel myself when it came to flaunting the rules. But whereas I always made it back in time for the various meetings or the prearranged trips, Nicolas was often absent. This caused our hosts to go crazy searching for him. When he finally did show, smiling broadly, they invariably seemed to forgive him. It was evident however, Nicolas had managed to cross some invisible line.

Nicolas continued: "Mr Kim told me that he was the guide for an Australian guy two years ago, who was also fond of disappearing by himself. It turned out that he was taking pictures which he later published in the West. Mr Kim was severely reprimanded, and so remains particularly careful nowadays. He must have reported me to Mr Sok. I have to meet Mr Sok at 10pm. They want to see my photos and videos. I could show them the videos but I don't want them to develop my films."

I offered to hide the films in my room.

We went about it like secret service agents in some old movie — me back to my room, and Nicolas knocking on my door a short while later, the films in a plastic bag.

"Seems nobody followed me," he said. "Here are the films... and some notes I made. Can you hide them as well?"

"Notes in French? They know I don't speak French. Oh, what the fuck. I'll do it."

It was about five minutes to ten, and our apprehension was mounting. The closer it got to the meeting with Mr Sok, the more the predicament we might have got ourselves into hit home. Here we were, seated in a darkened hotel room in Pyongyang, hoping that the place was too cheap to have surveillance equipment installed, and debating worst case scenarios. If Nicolas was handed over to the police, for instance.

"Give me the address of somebody who knows you well and who has contacts with the Western press," I said.

"My parents," responded Nicolas. "I'll give you my parents' address. Got a pen?"

I always have pens around, but at that moment couldn't find one. I rummaged through all my pockets and bags. Nothing.

"Can you remember Rue de..."

Soldiers at the Friendship Exhibition on Mount Myohyang, and (right) relaxing outside Pyongyang Station.
Photos: Christian Karl

"No, I can't," I snapped in frustration. "We've got to write it down."

Suddenly there came a knock on the door, followed by the voice of Mr Kim: "Mr Nicolas? Are you there? I'm looking for you."

I felt a pen in my trouser pocket — how come I didn't find it before?

"Write the address down," I whispered.

"Where?"

"Here, on this fucking Pyongyang postcard! Good luck, hope to see you later tonight!"

Nicolas opened the door and shuffled away with the waiting Mr Kim.

I went down to the bar. They were already switching off the lights, but I managed to buy some *sul* on the chance we had something to celebrate later tonight. Nicolas' return from the meeting would suffice for now.

The film export people had installed VCRs in our hotel rooms to enable us to continue with the "Korea Film Show" in the evenings. Unfortunately, the tapes they had given us contained no subtitles. The films seemed to be rather dreary, anyway, and I ended up fast forwarding through some of them. Occasionally I would switch to the TV, hoping to catch any news that didn't involve the sight of the marathon girl endlessly racing across the screen.

Eventually, a knock on the door.

"It's me. Nicolas."

I opened the door. Nicolas was alone, and grinning.

"So, what happened?" I asked.

"Nothing. Nothing at all. Mr Sok just wanted to talk about money. He showed me a contract that he had prepared, obliging me to sell some of their documentaries in Europe. The deal was very much in their favour, leaving me with nothing."

"Did you sign?"

"Of course not. But I might end up signing anything just to get out of here. I don't think the spy issue is resolved yet."

In the morning, as was customary, we had a meeting with Mr Paek, Mr Sok and our guides at the Korea Film Export and Import offices — conversations about nothing in particular over cups of instant coffee. Today started out no differently, until Mr Sok suddenly shifted gear: "Mr Nicolas, I saw you filming around the hotel on the day of your arrival. What did you film there?" Mr Sok elaborated. "There was nothing going on. You even filmed the backyard. Why did you do that?"

"What's wrong with that?" Nicolas responded.

"It is not the best hotel in Pyongyang and the backyard is not very beautiful." Probed Mr Sok, asking the question again: "So, why did you film it?"

"Yeah, the backyard is not great but it's not awful either. Just a backyard — nothing special."

"Why did you film it then?"

"Just to create some atmosphere on my tape. So that when I return home I can see what it was like being here."

"You sure that is the only reason? You also went out a lot on your own — taking a lot of cameras with you. What were you doing then?"

"Just walking around, taking pictures."

"Pictures? What for?"

"For myself."

"You know, our country has many enemies. Some of them pose as our friends. They take pictures of the bad parts of our country and sell them to magazines in South Korea. And you take pictures of bad things like the backyard of the hotel."

"No, no, no, no. I just take pictures of daily life. Good or bad, I don't care. I want to get shots of how people live."

"What for?"

"For me."

"I don't believe you," concluded Mr Sok. "May I see your photos and videos?"

"Sure you may. But you told me I could move around freely in your country. So what's the problem?"

Mr Paek, who had been smiling quietly on the sofa like a Buddha, interjected: "You may move around freely. But we have to watch what you are doing. To prevent you from making a mistake."

"What mistake?"

No answer followed. The topic was over for now... although Mr Paek's fresh line of conversation seemed suspiciously cognisant.

"Mr Nicolas, you were the head of the Swiss delegation at the last April Culture Festival and your delegation won the gold medal..."

"Yeah," interrupted Nicolas, "and I was on TV a lot, too, so why don't you trust me this time?"

Mr Paek ignored the question. "We want you to put together another delegation for next year's April Culture Festival. We need a solo flautist who has won at least one gold medal in an international competition in the field of classical music. We want..."

Mr Paek reeled off a list of musical demands, some by expertise and class, others by name. When he had finished, he asked, "You think you can get us those people?"

"Um, I'll try," answered Nicolas somewhat feebly. "Give me your list."

Now it was me they turned to.

"Can you recommend any international film magazines that could be helpful for us?"

"Sure. Get a hold of *Variety*, *Sight and Sound*, and *Film Comment*.

They're required reading."

"How can you help us with these?" I was asked.

"Well, I can get you the subscription addresses."

"But these publications are very expensive for us."

"Uh, well, I can send you my copies after reading them..."

This offer met with satisfaction, although Mr Paek added that I needn't bother sending *Variety* as they already subscribed to it. This was odd. Miss Choe worked full time in the offices of the film export company and spoke fluent English, but yet knew nothing of *Variety*. Mr Paek, however, who couldn't read a word of English, got the paper delivered to his desk. I realised these magazines were not meant to be read — they were simply to indicate hierarchic status; to show who was entrusted enough to inspect a Western publication and who wasn't...

We went to the movies.

Every visitor to North Korea must invite his or her hosts to one official meal. At lunchtime today, it was my turn. Miss Choe had arranged everything in advance: we went to the barbecue place near Kim Il Sung Square where we had been on our first night. The tables had typical Korean barbecue grills built into them — something I loved since my first encounter with Korean cuisine a few years earlier in New York. Alas, the ones here didn't work. We sat down and Mr Sok began to order. Mr Sok might have been the one handling the unpleasant stuff at the company, but at least he knew how to enjoy life. (Maybe all his schemes were geared towards him becoming the ambassador to France one day?)

The food was excellent and here I had my first encounter with Pyongyang-style cold buckwheat noodles. Great stuff!

Through the windows, on Kim Il Sung Square, I could see several thousand school children practising some kind of mass gymnastics display. I was informed that it was a rehearsal for celebrations taking place the following day, September 9, "the anniversary of the foundation of the Democratic People's Republic of Korea by our Great Leader Kim Il-sung."

In the midst of small talk about the food, Mr Sok turned to Nicolas and praised him for being such a talented cameraman. "Mr Nicolas," he said. "I would like to see some of your work."

"You saw some of my films at last year's festival," responded Nicolas.

"I think you have certainly improved your style since then," Mr Sok pressed on.

"I can send you some more recent videos when I get home."

"No, I want to see some of your works tonight. I feel a great urge to catch up on your artistic development."

"But I don't have any of my films here..."

"In that case, I would just watch the material you have shot so far while here."

"But that's not edited yet..."

"I have to evaluate the artistry of films all the time. I can tell if you are as talented as you seem to be."

"But that's just raw footage, nothing else. A lot will get thrown away."

"Do you invite me to see your films tonight?"

"Well, it's all on Hi8 and you don't have facilities to play Hi8."

"I will watch it on the camera viewfinder then, if you don't mind."

"But it's not art, just tourist footage..."

I jumped in: "Ah, right, tourist footage. I'm sure I'm in it."

Nicolas threw me a perplexed look.

"I'm sure I'm in it," I repeated. "We went around a lot together, didn't we? I want to see the footage, too. Do you invite me to the little screening tonight?"

Nicolas glanced over gratefully. "You don't mind do you, Mr Sok?"

A training session for the mass gymnastic display.
Photo: Christian Karl

"Uh-huh..." was Mr Sok's muffled reply.

Time now to see a few more big screen Juche heroes defending the fatherland.

That evening at the hotel restaurant, Mr Kim arrived to collect Nicolas. "Ah," I said, getting up from the dinner table, "the video show starts." "No," Mr Kim said politely. "Mr Sok wants to meet only with Mr

Nicolas. Maybe you can see the videos another time?"

Nicolas didn't look too happy but had no choice but to leave alone.

Meanwhile, I went back to my room to watch *Pulgasari*. Mr Paek insisted there was no print of this 1985 film available for the screening series, but Miss Choe had managed to get me a video tape of it. It's a North Korean Godzilla flick, set in medieval times. It was produced by none other than the Dear Leader Kim Jong-il himself, while its Southern director — Shin Sang-ok — always maintained that he'd been kidnapped in Hong Kong and taken to North Korea to make films! Having completed *Pulgasari*, Shin was allowed to go to Europe, whereupon he immediately asked for asylum at the American embassy in Vienna. Except for its theatrical run in Japan, the film remained banned.

I was amazed that nobody had balked at my attempts to order it.

The "Godzilla" in *Pulgasari* starts out as a little figure formed from half-chewed food by an old blacksmith in prison. The blacksmith dies and his daughter inherits the figure. One night, she injures herself with a sewing needle and a little drop of her blood falls onto the figure, causing it to come to life. The little figure immediately starts to eat all the iron it can find. The more iron it eats the bigger it becomes. Of course, this being a North Korean film, the creature is soon helping the poor in their fight against feudal lords. *Pulgasari* is given an impressive technical sheen courtesy of Japanese special-effects experts who had previously worked on "official" Godzilla movies. Neither was Kenpachiro Satsuma, the guy inside the Pulgasari costume, any stranger to monster destruction: he had smashed up Tokyo numerous times wearing the heavy Godzilla outfit. He even wrote a book — *North Korea Seen Through the Eyes of Godzilla*.

I had finally got to see the near legendary masterwork of trash I had read about — typically, though, without the help of subtitles. But I loved it!

When the movie was over, I decided to buy some *sul* and head over to Nicolas' room to see how the screening was going. Mr Kim opened the door. "Ah, Mr Johannes," he said. "What's up?"

"I thought I might join your little video party now."

"Please come in," responded Mr Kim, for wont of anything else to say.

Mr Sok was peering intensely into a camera viewfinder, but relaxed and leaned back when I walked in. "Yes, you are very talented, Mr Nicolas," he said. "I knew from the beginning. Very good work."

Mr Sok joined us in a glass of *sul*, cracking a few jokes that bore no relation to the videos at all. Then he headed off, claiming he had "a lot of work to do".

Yeah — writing reports on us, probably.

Mr Kim was happy to bag some big bars of Swiss chocolate and a picture book on Geneva before he made his exit.

With both of them gone, Nicolas erupted into laughter. "I'm so happy you came over! Once you arrived, the atmosphere changed completely." Nicolas leaned over. "You know how it had been before? Pure horror! I had to show them the same scenes over and over again. Each time they asked the same questions: 'Why did you take this shot? Why that? Are you a spy? What are you going to do with the pictures?' In the end I thought they might just take all the tapes — and ask where the photos were."

"What would you have said about the photos?"

"I already prepared some fakes. It worked in fooling Lao border guards; it would work here, too. They would end up developing unexposed films and I would make a big show of it. *'You fuckers, you fucked up my films! No pictures left after you had them in your stupid fingers!'* Just like in Laos..."

We both had our own pet theories on the background to these accusations. Nicolas held the opinion that Mr Kim had to make good for his mistake of two years ago with the Australian photographer. Mr Sok also wanted to finger a spy in order to secure a promotion at work, moving up from his current job. I thought differently. The only reason Nicolas was being accused and not me was that I simply had better luck with my hosts. Mr Paek already held a good position, and it was he who had found that one odd European — me — wanting to show North Korean films in the West. Miss Choe on the other hand was a humble translator; she was simply happy to meet somebody from the outside.

I had a relatively easy time. Nicolas was stuck with desperate men.

Mr Sok was in charge of making film rights deals with Western Europe, had gone to Paris a few times, and certainly enjoyed life there. But he always came back from Paris empty-handed. So he had invited Nicolas as a kind of counterweight to Mr Paek having invited me. But Nicolas turned out not to be in the business Sok had assumed, namely film distribution. Further embarrassment to Sok. He had probably already taken some heat from Paek on that issue. After all, Korea Film Export had paid our expenses here. And to cap it all, Nicolas had created extra friction in being caught running around alone with lots of cameras.

Both our theories, of course, boiled down to the same thing: Kim was scared and would report every little detail, and Sok was ruthless when it came to trying to achieve his goals. But so long as they didn't get the police involved, there was no real danger — only the pressure and tedium of being under virtual house-arrest.

It was the DPRK (Democratic People's Republic of Korea) founding day and national holiday — but no break for us. We had to continue watching movies all day long, in the spirit of the "Shock Brigades" who knew no holidays either. We had seen plenty of Shock Brigades in the movies and occasionally on the streets, too: young volunteers, building bridges, highways and high-rises. I loved the Shock Brigade girls in their cute uniforms, and I went around playfully admonishing everyone, *"Shock Brigade spirit! No breaks! More movies!"*

The export company people didn't seem to possess much of that spirit, though. They wanted one rest after another. And they got them — the screenings were often interrupted by power failures.

"That's due to the American imperialists," Miss Choe explained. "We couldn't build our own nuclear power station because of them. They promised to help us build light-water reactors but so far they haven't done anything."

Once the screenings were over for the day, we were taken to the big celebration on Kim Il Sung Square. Here, lack of electrical power wasn't an issue. The roofs of the buildings were covered with thousands of flood lights, the brightly lit Juche Tower rising forth on the other side of the river. Having seen the children rehearsing, I was expecting a gigantic mass gymnastics display. There wasn't one. There weren't even any speeches.

On the streets of
Pyongyang.
Photos: Christian Karl

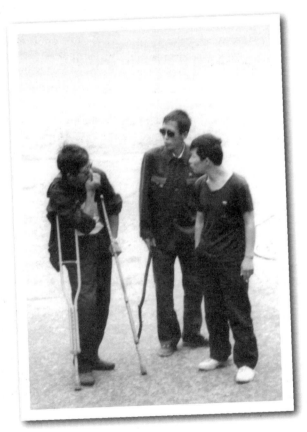

Maybe these things had taken place earlier in the day?

Although the music was the same awful revolutionary music as always, all in all it was quite a joyous party. Along with all the other foreigners in town — who ranged from tourists to diplomats, a meagre 200 or so in total — we were placed on the right side of the large stone stand overlooking the square. Behind us was the Grand People's Study House, Pyongyang's main library, which had its own balcony. It was from here that Kim Jong-il would occasionally watch parades or celebrations like this one — although he rarely ever showed up.

Down on the square, women in traditional Korean garb danced in little circles around poles decorated with colourful ribbons. It didn't look like much rehearsal had gone into this particular display. People just seemed to be having a good time. After a short while, the dancing circles dissipated and the participants were simply dancing freely with one another. We could join in, if we wanted. Nicolas did, having a few rounds with Miss Choe.

The party was still in full swing when Mr Sok urged us to return to the hotel.

We walked off Kim Il Sung Square through an unlit side street — the city outside of the celebration being as dark as it ever was. We encountered military vehicles and security forces blocking off the street, but were able to walk around them without any problem or questions asked. However, sporadic fist fights broke out between security staff and several young men not long after we did so. Fierce fights, as far one could tell in the darkness. I wondered whether the confrontation was due to common citizens being refused access to the festivities.

"What about those fights?" I asked Miss Choe. "Is it people trying to get in or out?"

"What fights?" she replied. "There are no fights."

"There *are* fights. Can't you see them?" I insisted, pointing at the battle closest to us.

"Ah, you mean that," she sighed. "That's not fighting. Just a little... pushing for discipline."

Nicolas left his camera case closed.

Our final day in Pyongyang. We got off to an early start, paying the customary visit to the eternal president Kim Il-sung in his state of eternal silence.

I had already seen Lenin lying dead, stuffed in his Moscow mausoleum, and this was like a visit to a bygone era. I recalled Red Square being cordoned off. At a checkpoint visitors were searched for cameras, and then ushered along a line of solemn policemen into the chilly display room. Loitering was prohibited and one had to walk by the exhibit quickly. Lenin was dressed in a suit from the 1920s. It all felt a little shabby. One could also visit the gravestones along the Kremlin wall, of Stalin, Khrushchev and Brezhnev. Following this visit with ghosts of the past, it was quite cool to have lunch at a Western burger bar on the other side of Red Square, where the new times had set in.

I had also seen Mao in his Beijing display room. No cameras were allowed there either, but the protocol was far less spartan than in Moscow. One could buy flowers to lay nearby, or a little information booklet on the mausoleum. Dressed in his Mao suit and covered by a Chinese flag, visitors were still required to walk by the Great Helmsman quickly (or the wax puppet stand-in when the original Mao was undergoing restoration). The whole purpose of the exhibition seemed to be channelled toward the big souvenir shop situated behind the display room, in which every imaginable item of Mao kitsch was available: from Mao cigarette lighters (which played the tune of 'The East is Red' whenever in use), to Mao posters, postcards, cups, plates and lamps. There were Mao sculptures of all sizes and even Mao tea. Once through the exit, hundreds of stalls offered the Mao pilgrim everything from batteries to umbrellas, rolls of photographic films to Mickey Mouse T-shirts.

The Kumsusang Memorial Palace is a totally different affair. Hun-

Kumsusan Memorial Hall, the Kim Il-sung mausoleum.
Photo: Christian Karl

dreds of people lined up in orderly fashion at the front entrance. No individual visitors but rather army platoons, farmer co-operatives and factory-worker units. As always the foreigners were led to the front of the line. The actual "palace" was quite a distance away from the main entrance. There was a long passageway to traverse, after first walking over a blanket of brushes to disperse any dirt being brought in. Then it was necessary to place any cameras and metal objects into storage. A metal detector and a body search followed. Foreign coins, aluminium-wrap cigarette packets — anything metallic that we had neglected to relinquish earlier — were then removed and taken to the storage desk by our guides. We were transported by a moving walkway to the actual palace. We had no option but to remain on it — walking was prohibited. The walkway proceeded very slowly, in order to give us time to "collect our thoughts", as Miss Choe put it.

Once inside the marble palace, we were led into the room where the Great Leader stood — or rather, a big stone statue of him, in front of which we had to bow. Revolutionary music played; everything was very solemn. Following another cleansing procedure — this one blowing dust from our clothes and dry scalp off our heads via cold jets of air — we were ushered into the holy room where Kim Il-sung's eternity was resting. In the centre was the holiest shrine in North Korea: Kim Il-sung himself, under glass, dressed in a suit. It was required that we see him from all sides, always stopping and bowing to him.

Behind us was a class of school girls, about fourteen-years-old, most of them crying. Even Miss Choe shed a little tear upon seeing the Great Leader, motionless and smiling.

An exhibition room contained the Great Leader's personal Mercedes 600, and the railway car in which he had travelled as far as East Berlin. (An illuminated map of all his routes adorned one wall.) There were the medals and honorary doctorates he had received from around the world — mostly Eastern Europe's now defunct Communist states and former Asian Communist countries; he was a "honorary citizen" in pretty much every Peruvian small town controlled by the Sendero Luminoso guerrilla movement, and also in a lot of Italian villages whose mayors were Communist. There was even a document of "honourable membership" from a US based International Student Association. This item looked particularly pompous, but on closer inspection revealed a liberal use of correction fluid — obviously the creation of students with a sense of humour. It probably netted them the red carpet treatment in Pyongyang.

We had to use the moving walkways again on the way out, but this time without the instruction to "collect out thoughts".

Back at the film export office, the final contracts were presented to Nicolas and myself for signing — separately. While Nicolas was signing his shitty legal document, I was given a movie to watch, and vice versa.

I had made the decision to take ten features and four short documentaries on my tour through Europe in the spring. Examining the paperwork, however, I saw that there were only nine films listed. I checked through my own notes to see what was missing.

"What's up?" Mr Paek asked.

"I had decided on ten films but there's only nine on the list," I replied.

"Oh, we took *Pulgasari* out."

"Why?"

"Um…" Mr Paek looked to Miss Choe, who said something in Korean to him. "Ah yes," Mr Paek continued, "the negative got destroyed."

"I don't want the negative, I just want a print."

"Sorry, not possible."

I signed the fucking paper, even though I felt that without *Pulgasari* — the missing movie — the tour would be severely lacking. Still, I got a whole bunch of over-the-top propaganda pictures and some fairly good action movies that nobody had ever screened in Western Europe before.

The rest of the day was spent shopping for "Korean handicrafts", which turned out to be the worst tourist kitsch imaginable. Gazing incredulously at an embroidery of the Mona Lisa, Nicolas and I cracked a few jokes. This prompted Mr Kim to come over and check what we were up to.

"Nothing," we replied.

Worried, he looked at the European face on the embroidery. "Who is that?" he asked.

"That's the Mona Lisa — about the most famous painting in the world. You've never heard of it before?"

"No." His response was curt.

We went to a store selling postage stamps, where a true philatelist could easily part with all his money. The North Koreans had stamps that featured pretty much anything and everything: twenty-five years of Lufthansa, an anniversary of Daimler Benz, and so on.

Eventually, we wound up at a department store, in which we were the only customers. Nicolas felt like buying a can of the Chinese orange juice that filled the New York deli-style refrigerators. That was a problem.

"Sorry, we cannot sell that juice," one of the sales assistants said from behind the counter.

"Why not?"

"Because..."

We bartered like this for some minutes, until a sales lady offered conclusively: "It's freshly imported. The price is not fixed yet."

Clearly the orange juice was for decoration and not for sale at all.

"What about a beer?" one of the assistants asked.

Nicolas bought a bottle of Chinese Yanjin beer but didn't want to drink alone. Half-joking he asked for glasses. No problem. The ladies brought out a set of cognac glasses that had been on display, split the bottle of beer between ourselves and our guides and watched us drink at their desk in the empty store.

Over dinner, Nicolas and I talked about just one thing: how great it would be to get the hell out of here. The Yugoslavian couple — here to train basketball players — leaned over and made a few envious comments. Sasha — the alcoholic Russian — failed one last time to get us up to his room for drinks. The video equipment from mine and Nicolas' rooms had already been removed by a film export technician.

We were driven to the airport in the film export company's van. Nicolas held a video camera out the window through the entire journey. This didn't pose any problem with our hosts — all he could see was the road that all important guests of the state use, which was maintained appropriately. When we suddenly encountered a public bus with engine failure and some fifty or so people trying to push it up a hill, Miss Choe clapped her hand over the lens of Nicolas' camera.

"There is nothing to see," she said.

The airport was hectic with everyone seemingly in a hurry to leave the country. Most of the faces I had seen on the flight arriving were now here, leaving as well. Like us, they all had the standard eight-day visa.

After checking in our luggage we went upstairs. Although smoking was permitted pretty much everywhere in North Korea, there was no smoking allowed in the airport — excepting a little bar from which I observed Mr Sok delivering one last admonishment to Nicolas. As I rejoined them, I caught the guide's last words: "You should always be sure, Mr Nicolas, that I have eyes in Switzerland, too."

We arrived at Beijing Airport — which was reason enough to celebrate! I took a bottle of Ryongssang beer from my bag and drank it with Nicolas in front of the airport's glass doors. Free again! Mr Sok suddenly seemed no more intimidating than a ludicrous cartoon figure!

Later that day, I made the long walk from the city centre to the China Trade Centre and its internet café. It felt great deciding for myself when and where I should eat, whether or not I should take this road or that...

Part 2

I premiered my series of North Korean feature films at the Gothenburg Film Festival in Sweden in January 2000, followed by screenings at the Udine Far East Film Festival in Italy and a couple of cinemas in Germany. It was hard to convince cinema and festival bookers to show the programme at all — most bookers refused to believe that North Korean films would be of any interest to the public. Since most of the films were without subtitles, I had to drive to all the venues myself and provide them with a digital subtitle display machine that I had rented from the Turkish Film Festival people in Nuremberg.

Press comments varied greatly. Sweden's largest daily, *Dagens Nyheter,* accused the Gothenburg Film Festival of showing 'state-pro-

North Korean Films in Europe, Spring 2000

duced lies without comment'; Hong Kong's *Asiaweek* stated that the films 'looked like they come from another planet'; London's *Economist* wrote that the films 'allowed the free world to confirm its worst fears about that troubled land'; Berlin *Tip* magazine deduced that there was 'nothing more decadent these days than watching North Korean hero epics — while the country itself starved to death'.

One excited Munich headline read simply: 'Views into a Rogue State.'

In short, it was a success with the press and — in spite of the bookers' fears — with audiences as well. But in the end the tour made no money whatsoever.

Nicolas got the April Culture Festival two classical musicians, but didn't travel with them to Pyongyang.

In June 2000, the first-ever summit meeting between South Korean President Kim Dae-jung and Great Leader Kim Jong-il took place in Pyongyang. North Korea was in the world's headlines, and a thaw between the old enemies seemed imminent. Following the summit, there was a lot of official activity as delegations moved between Pyongyang and Seoul; people were allowed to meet relatives on the other side of the Demilitarised Zone — the most heavily fortified border in the world — and South Korea released a group of imprisoned Communist spies back into their homeland, North Korea.

Forever In Our Memory and *Woman Warrior of Koryo* (next page), two of the films the author screened as part of his North Korea programme.

Pulgasari was screened in Seoul, South Korea, in Summer 2000. It opened in five theatres but closed after one week, having drawn less than 1,000 people. The film was considered the worst box-office failure of the year. South Korean teens and young adults — constituting the biggest part of

the cinema audience — were evidently not interested in the low-tech campiness of the picture, according to the South Korean press. More likely, though, nobody showed up because there is no Godzilla cult tradition in South Korea, thanks to the government having prohibited the import of all Japanese films right up until 1999. In Japan, the home of Godzilla, *Pulgasari* did very well.

I finally got to eat dog meat in Pusan, South Korea. Everyone in the traditional Korean restaurant was keen to hear what I thought of it, not having had a foreign customer for a couple of years. When I began to praise it they seemed immensely proud. It's great meat!

Part 3

The Seventh Pyongyang Film Festival of Non-Aligned and Other Developing Countries, Sept 2000

In Summer 2000, Mr Paek and Mr Sok came to Berlin. We had a brief meeting at the "Office for the Protection of the Interests..." where they asked me to put together a big delegation for the Pyongyang Film Festival to be held in September.

I tried my best, inviting people from as far as Tokyo to join in, but not many found the idea of going to North Korea particularly appealing. One American writer and distributor wrote back to me, saying, "This sounds like the worst idea since the Kursk* went out on manoeuvres."

In the end I managed to pull a delegation together consisting of six Germans, not all of them involved in film. Christian from Berlin was dabbling as a freelance journalist and hoping to shoot some great photos in North Korea. Kay was a drug counsellor from Nuremberg who had a special interest in Commie kitsch. On the cinema side there was Mark from the Kommunales Kino in Leipzig (who not only screened my series at his theatre, but had a South Korean girlfriend and spoke a little Korean), Alice from the Munich Werkstattkino (which had also screened the programme), and film dealer Daniel of Kirch Media, the German equivalent of Time Warner (who had been one of the biggest fans of the programme when it played in Munich).

Daniel was the only one of the group with the potential to make any sizeable deal with the North Koreans.

Christian, Kay and I travelled together to Beijing, where we met up with Nicolas. The original plan was to continue to Pyongyang by train, a plan I had confirmed with Mr Paek. Although our visas allowed us to visit Sinuiju, the North Korean border town which is the crossing point for trains, we couldn't buy any tickets in Beijing. "The train is fully booked, it has only two passenger cars crossing the border," the main Chinese travel agency told us. Well, that might have been true — but I had also heard that the train often doesn't run at all due to fuel shortages in North Korea.

We could have gone to Dandong, the Chinese border town, and tried our luck on black market tickets, but if that failed our whole visit would be in jeopardy. So we tried the Air Koryo office instead. To our huge surprise they already had all the names of the delegates, and were expecting us!

The North Koreans don't leave anything to chance.

We were flying over that great vacant highway once again, and I was looking forward to a big celebration like last year — perhaps we would be the stars this time? But the film festival delegates didn't get the reception that had greeted the marathon girl. Instead, we were filtered away from the rest of the passengers, put onto a bus and driven over to the reception committee, which consisted of Mr Choe, the head of Korea Film Export (no relation to Miss Choe), two vice-something-or-others, and some press. Miss Choe was also there to greet the German delegates, as was Miss Pak, whom I had met only briefly the previous year. The two of them would be our guides this time.

The search at customs for mobile phones was more intensive this year. With that out of the way, the whole group of international festival guests — totalling around forty, along with their guides — boarded two buses. The largest group from Europe was represented by the Germans. There were two guys from Finland, only here because they had acted upon Mr Paek's fax number I had given to them at the Pusan Film Festival in South Korea ("You are to blame for us being here," the Fins now accused me jokingly). Nicolas was back, the one-person delegation from Switzerland. There was a group of Russians, although two of the Russian delegates turned out to be Germans who ran the Moscow studio for Germany's ZDF TV — they wanted to use the occasion to get some TV material on North Korea. There were also small delegations from Iran, Vietnam, Japan, China, Cambodia and Malaysia.

A lot of the expected delegations never arrived. "Where is Nigeria? Where is Algeria? Where is Senegal? Where is Poland?" queried the guides over and over again.

Nicolas told me that there had been a lot more guests at the last festival, no less than a hundred in fact.

This time we were staying at the twin-tower Koryo Hotel, the most international if not best hotel in Pyongyang. On the thirtieth floor, I had a great view of the city, my window opening directly onto the

*The Russian submarine which sank in the Barents Sea, with all on board perishing.

pyramid ruin that was the Ryongyong Hotel. The first day was free for the guests. We could do whatever we wanted — except leave the hotel, that is. The German and Finnish delegations however, headed out together a little after 10pm in search of a bar — maybe the barbecue joint on Kim Il Sung Square? Nicolas was having problems with his guide and couldn't join us.

We walked through the dark streets. Nothing appeared to be open. We eventually found the restaurant, but that too was closed. Even the Juche tower got switched off at 10pm. But there was a crowd of several thousand school children hanging around Kim Il Sung Square. Having nothing better to do we decided to stick around and see what was going on. Fired into animation by a loud distorted voice ringing through a speaker system, the children suddenly all got up and raced into position for a mass gymnastics display. Thousands of children running this way and that, with us in the middle — we made a quick break for the stone stands. From this vantage point we were close to the woman barking orders and directing the games.

At least 10,000 kids were going through hard training in the middle of the night, brandishing short metal sticks in the shape of the calligraphy

Kim Il Sung Square at night with mass gymnastics training session.
Photo: Christian Karl

brush that was the party symbol for the arts. They repeated the same moves over and over, under the scrutiny and command of the female chieftain. We eventually got bored, went back to the hotel and sat in its revolving bar which overlooked the entire city. The only place still illuminated below us was Kim Il Sung Square, the kids continuing with their rehearsals way beyond the bar's closing time. As we discovered the next day, they kept at it until 3am, having to be back at school the following morning. It turned out they were preparing for the fifty-fifth anniversary celebrations of the Workers Party — the Communist party of North Korea — which were being held on October 10. These nocturnal rehearsals had been taking place since November of the previous year.

Our morning was spent visiting the giant Kim Il-sung statue. It was a considerably larger event this time with the North Korean delegates carrying a banner that read: "Comrade Kim Il-sung is always alive in the hearts of humanity!" As the head of the German delegation, I had the honour of placing the flowers down myself. After that, we were taken to the birthplace of Kim Il-sung — a couple of little huts functioning as another holy place. A group of heavily tattooed Australian teenagers in Heavy Metal T-shirts were there, possibly on some kind of shock trip to scare juvenile delinquents away from further crime.

Parade outside the Pyongyang International Cinema Hall.
Photo: Christian Karl

Lunch break at the hotel. Nicolas was fighting with his guide again, so the Germans and Fins went out without him to the department store on the corner — which was empty but for the sales ladies. A few items were on display, but all of it arranged in such a fashion that made it impossible to take one item out without bringing the whole lot crashing down. I wanted to buy a bottle of fruit juice but was pointed in the direction of the hotel by the sales assistants — we would be served there.

Apparently, it was just another exhibition of goods not for sale.

We got thrown out of the train station, then took some photos of commuters in the little park nearby, awaiting trains to take them to their homes in the countryside. Really poor people it seemed, much worse off than those living in Pyongyang itself, and noticeably malnourished. In 1999, I hadn't seen anyone who looked malnourished; now I did. There were a few little street stalls selling food. Lots of food — *Kimbap* (Korean sushi) and all kinds of baked goods. But with prices from five won upwards, nobody was buying. If Miss Choe made 200

won a month, as she had once told me, and she was certainly in a lot better a position financially than these folks, how could anybody afford to pay such prices? I tried to buy some pastries but the stall holders wouldn't sell me any — I had foreign blue won and they accepted only regular peoples' brown won.

Unlike the department stores, at least they *had* something to sell.

A lot of children ran away when they saw Christian's camera, although the older folks didn't seem to care. Some guards got angry, however, and chased him off when he tried to photograph a fire burning rubbish in a school yard.

Although we had seen people on every public square all over town rehearsing mass gymnastic displays, it wasn't the case in this particular vicinity, where the people were apparently too low class to participate.

We were on our way back to the hotel when we ran into a breathless and somewhat exasperated Miss Pak. "I'm so happy to find you!" she coughed. "The celebrations are earlier than expected — we have to get to the bus right now. Where have you been?"

The bus took us to the huge Pyongyang International Cinema Hall on Yanggak Islet on the Taedong River. We were dropped off quite far from the entrance, and greeted by the female brass band of the Korean Peoples' Army. They led the way to the cinema complex as we marched behind them, soon flanked on both sides by thousands of girls in traditional costume. Most danced with colourful fans, while others danced with large sheets of bright cloth or drummed on old-style changgos. Another cutely dressed female unit played Western-style drums. All this for us, a few foreigners!

And yet there were no members of the public watching the event — just a small army of North Korean newsmen.

Arriving finally at the steps leading up to the entrance, we were greeted by 'young pioneers'* in uniform. They greeted us with well-rehearsed speeches in Korean and English, then rushed towards us and presented us with flowers. We entered the building.

Much of the audience was already there, virtually filling the 2,000 seat cinema. The show started promptly. Accompanied by a live classical orchestra, the first film was an ostentatious effort hailing the success of previous festivals, narrated in that North Korean female voice that's so weirdly distinctive. A strange sing-song, it falls somewhere between a sports commentary and a chanting priest. They praise all "achievements" in North Korean documentaries with this kind of a voice, and the guides at places like the Kim Il-sung mausoleum invariably adopt the same manner of speaking as well.

I spotted Nicolas up on the screen, running around as usual with his camera.

*Young pioneers is the name for members of the Communist Youth organisation in all Communist countries. I was a young pioneer as a child in East Germany. Young pioneers wear red scarves.

Young pioneers (previous page) and various dance troupes constitute the Film Festival 2000 reception. *Photos: Christian Karl and J Schönherr*

North Korean
'revolutionary' attire.
Photo: Christian Karl

Speeches followed and the guests of honour were called to the stage, amongst them the Egyptian Vice Minister of Culture. What the hell was he doing here? Nowhere to be seen however was the great movie lover and film producer himself, Kim Jong-il — he doesn't even attend his own film festival!

An Iranian film director gave the final speech, commemorating the international cinema community and the foreign film workers who comprised tonight's guests. He seemed uncomfortable and nervous. Both his hands gripped the text of his speech, and shook as he read. He told me later that he hadn't actually written a single word of the speech, but had been given it by the North Koreans who insisted that he read it.

We filed out of the ceremony, got onto our buses and were taken immediately to the next official function — at the fabled Ongryu Restaurant, hailed as the "best restaurant of North Korea" and legendary home of Pyongyang cold noodles. I was thrilled, expecting the best cold noodles of my life.

We dined in the main assembly hall. The minister for culture gave a short speech, after which we headed over to the tables and our fixed seating arrangement. Alice from the Werkstattkino, Miss Choe, Mr Sok and three officials sat at my large round table — much too large for us to talk comfortably to one another. One of the officiates introduced himself as the mastermind behind today's festivities at the cinema hall. His two associates remained silent throughout the evening, which relegated the difficult conversation at the table to just small talk among the guests and their guides.

I could see Kay debating excitedly with an old official at the next table. They were arguing over the details of Mao suits, with Kay trying to get hold of the address of the official party tailor.

The food was disappointing. Much worse than the food we had tasted the previous year in far humbler restaurants, and no match for Korean restaurants in South Korea, Japan or even Berlin. Not enough spices — Korean food of course needing a lot of spices.

Was the fact that even ministers had to do without spices a sign of the economy declining yet further? Upon returning to Japan after my previous Pyongyang trip, I had been full of praise for North Korean cuisine. But this time...?

The cold noodles however — always served at the end of a meal — finally arrived, and they were exceptional. The South Korean journalists had been right: whenever they wrote about the summit meeting between their president and Kim Jong-il, there was always space enough to praise Pyongyang cold noodles.

Dinner was almost through. Miss Pak came over and whispered something to Miss Choe. Somehow, I guessed what it was about. Sure enough, Miss Choe asked me immediately afterwards what I had been doing at the train station. "You went there twice," she said.

"Just going out for a walk," I replied. "Nothing special."

"You know the rules here," she reprimanded. "No walking around without your guide. Ask me when you want to go somewhere — and please tell that to your delegates."

Oh, yeah, I was the head of the German delegation...

Back at the hotel, I asked the Fins if they had received any new instructions from their guide. They hadn't. Their guide spoke hardly any English and didn't really seem to care much about what they did.

It came as no surprise to discover soon after that the Fins would be getting a replacement guide.

Every delegation had one or two guides, depending on its size. Nicolas had a guide all to himself, a young man named Mr Kim, just like his guide from last time. (That Mr Kim was now in Beijing, helping coordinate the festival from there.) Nicolas would buy him drinks constantly to keep him drunk, but it didn't help much — Mr Kim was an ardent little watchdog, leaving Nicolas no room to do much on his own at all. Mr Sok, however, seemed to have forgotten all about the trouble he had had with Nicolas the previous year. He was constantly talking to Nicolas about "making money" and signing a new contract similar to the one last year — which had, of course, come to nothing.

The film festival finally got underway. The first morning, *Myself in Distant Future* had been chosen for us, to be screened away from the regular crowds in a small room at the cinema hall. I had shown that film in Europe and seen it at least thirty times. I knew the dialogue by heart and could even recite it. I was allowed to skip the screening.

I went to the film market on the second floor of the cinema hall — except there was no marketing taking place. There were only a couple of posters on the walls, several empty chairs and a few vacant video booths. If one was prepared to go through a mass of red tape it was possible to sample some North Korean videos. But no foreign delegations were bothering trying to sell their films in return. Who would they have sold them to, anyway? I was glad to discover the Fins loitering around — at least I wasn't the only one attending the "film market".

For the rest of the day, the entire German delegation were forced to watch the official "market programme," which consisted of tedious North Korean garbage that I would never have included in my own film series.

At least Mr Paek could sympathise, and offered to let us watch films — of any type we might actually want to see — over at the export company's office. Nevertheless, I had my own special request: I wanted to see a film, any film, inside the Taedongmun cinema. Having seen pictures of it and driven by it several times the previous year — when it was "unfortunately not possible" to go inside — I had wanted to visit the attractive little fifties' style film house with its faux Greek columns out front. This time my wish was granted.

The Taedongmun cinema was the first stop for the German delegation the following morning. A very nice little cinema indeed, although much bigger inside than the façade outside indicated. It was packed with locals — no foreigners around except for us, nor any delegations from factory or farm collectives. Just regular people, most wearing a uniform of some sort or another, as was the case in the streets.

Crash Landing was playing, a Chinese action film and quite a rarity for audiences here. North Korean cinemas don't show foreign productions outside the festival at all — thus Pyongyangites only had the opportunity to see foreign films once every two years. Outside of that, the only other foreign picture — mostly old and of Eastern European origin — came via a weekly slot on TV, accompanied by the once-a-week only broadcast of international news.

There were, however, some more well-to-do North Koreans we spoke with who had seen all the recent American blockbusters, courtesy of a large black market for bootlegs imported from China.

On the way to a mass gymnastics training session. Photo: Christian Karl

Crash Landing was shown with Korean voice-overs. Miss Pak translated to the two delegates sitting to her immediate left, of which I wasn't one — though that didn't hinder my understanding of what was happening in the film: an airplane is unable to drop its landing gear, the only alternative being to slide the craft down the runway and hope that the whole thing doesn't explode into a ball of flame. We see the crew taking all the necessary precautions, the ground staff preparing for the worst, and some passengers going nuts. Of course, the plane makes it down safely in the end.

The reaction of the audience was that of any other action film audience. Though, for me, leaving the theatre was far more like wandering into a weird movie than actually being in the cinema for nearly two hours. To see the inside of an Air China plane on the screen was nothing special; North Korean reality, however, after the lights came up, comprised of people passing by the theatre clutching huge flagpoles, children marching behind them, and soldiers everywhere. The whole city focused on the one collective task: preparing for the all-important Party anniversary.

More films at the export company offices. First up was *The Laudable Daughter of Korea,* a documentary about Jong Song-ok, the marathon girl of last year. We saw the award-winning run, her reception in Pyongyang, and the Mercedes and house she received from Kim Jong-il as a "thank you" — though the Great Leader didn't actually bother to meet her in person. We also saw Nicolas and myself, standing in the midst of a cheering crowd, and described by the narrator as a foreign TV crew. Ha! Breaking the rules, running away from our guides and still winding up as propaganda fodder! We should run away a lot more often, seeing as such behaviour was condoned by state propaganda!

Film studio main building (above) and, inside, the 'European Street' set.

Next page: Painting of the filming of *Sea of Blood,* inside the entrance hall of the Korean Film Studio.
Photo: Christian Karl

I had always wanted to see the place from whence these films came — the Korean Film Studios. In fact, North Korea has several film studios, among them the "April 25 Film Studio of the Korean Peoples' Army" and the "April 26 Children's Film Studio". But the Korean Film Studio was the biggest and most important. It was the true home of North Korean film, having been founded in 1947, and seeing production of the first North Korean film — *My Home Village* — in 1949. Last year I had inquired about a visit but was told, not unexpectedly, that such a thing was "unfortunately not possible".

This time a tour of the Korean Film Studios was part of the official festival programme. In preparation for the visit, each delegate received a booklet entitled *Great Man and Cinema*. I read mine on the bus on route to the studio — a collection of stories whose intent was to depict the Great Leader Kim Jong-il as a "master thinker, theoretician and leader of cinematic art and a benevolent and intimate father of film workers". In actuality, though, it chronicled the many horror stories of a powerful movie mogul who treated everyone around him like shit.

According to the booklet, even as a seven-year-old, Kim was a brat who interfered with the production of *My Home Village*. Later on, mid-production in other films, he would arrive unannounced and demand that crews change the way they were shooting, change the editing, and so on.

Old-style Hollywood studio heads like Jack Warner were notorious for dictatorial behaviour, but even they paled next to Kim Jong-il. Indeed, what was one to make of the following reference in *Great Man and Cinema*?

> When actors balked at piercing old people with their bayonets and throwing children into the fire, [the Great Leader] told them they should act with boldness to lend realism to the film.

We arrived at the studio, a large compound outside of Pyongyang. A huge painting of Kim Jong-il — overlooking the production of a battle scene in *Sea of Blood* — filled an entire wall in the lobby. His presence would be firmly felt during the first part of our studio tour. A female guide, with the customary exhortative sing-song voice, led us through a grand exhibition in which every chair and desk utilised by the Great One during his frequent "on-the-spot-guidance visits" were displayed from under glass — as were all cameras, film processing equipment, tape recorders, and floodlights that he had ever laid a hand upon. A visit by this guy must have been a nightmare, robbing the studio of much of its equipment! I asked about the films he had actually produced but the guide denied that the Great Leader was involved in any such activity.

"He only gave guidance and taught the people," I was informed. I knew that *Pulgasari* had been one of his vanity productions, however, at least according to the film's director, Shin Sang-ok. But as Shin had fled the country, I couldn't possibly present him as a reliable source for any argument to the contrary.

The Kim Jong-il exhibit finally behind us, we toured the mock location streets. There was a rural old-fashioned Korean street, a South Korean street (which didn't look like South Korea at all), a Japanese street (which didn't look like Japan at all), and a Western street (which could barely pass as being someplace on the furthest reaches of small-town, East Germany).

None of the set designers seemed to have appreciated that cities outside of North Korea had changed considerably in the last fifty years.

A simulated production staged for visitors was taking place in one of the huts of the "old Korean street". A medieval scene. Miss Choe introduced me to the main actor. For wont of anything better to discuss, I asked him how Kim Kil-in was doing. Kim Kil-in was the director of *Hong Kil Dong*, a sword-fight drama set in medieval times which happened to be one of my favourite films from North Korea, as well as one of the most successful during my European tour. Whenever I asked Miss Choe about the possibility of talking to the director, she steadfastly maintained that Kim Kil-in was "too busy". To my surprise, the actor told me that Kim Kil-in had actually died three years ago, "in the middle of shooting a film."

We were ushered into a meeting with (still living) North Korean movie people. I was introduced to some actresses from films I had screened in Europe, but the meeting was so brief that it wasn't possible to have more than a few fleeting words with any of them.

We were soon to discover that our fellow guests at the Koryo Hotel were the heroic "unconverted long-time prisoners"* of the South Koreans, recently returned to the North. I would occasionally run into one or two of them in the elevator, and we could sometimes see them being herded onto a bus.

Waiting for our own bus in front of the Koryo Hotel that afternoon, ready to go once again to the film export cinema, the "unconverted" arrived from some earlier visit on the doorstep of the hotel. Grey-haired old men all of them, each with a big medal on his jacket. One, who was confined to a wheelchair, suddenly came over to me and handed me a bunch of flowers. I stood rooted, a little surprised, as he sped off into the hotel. His comrades began to follow suit, handing flowers to all the foreigners.

At that moment, a commotion from within the hotel spilled out into the street. A member of staff was chasing a young man. The youth managed to give his pursuer the slip only to run headlong into a dozen plainclothed hotel guards. With a flurry of kicks and punches, the youth tried like a wild animal to resist being overpowered, but soon the guards had him pressed up against a wall. The fugitive wore his hair very short, was wrapped in an old blue jacket and bore a glare of such utter hatred that it brought a chill to the spine. Was he an example of North Korea's officially non-existent juvenile delinquents? Had he slipped into the hotel to try and steal something, knowing the severity of the punishment that awaited him and driven to avoid being caught at any cost?

A police car drove up, and the hotel guards helped the two officers pry the youth into their vehicle. They managed eventually and sped him away.

This time Miss Choe had no explanation.

According to numerous sources, the treatment of prisoners in North Korean labour camps — where people are interned for far less serious violations than trying to steal from an international hotel — are among the worst of the world, and the survival rate within them is poor. On the other hand, nobody really knows anything about actual crime rates in North Korea — which could be rather high when one considers all of the people going without food in the countryside.

Nicolas and I couldn't stay for the final celebrations of the festival as we had to be back in Europe. Not that we expected any more surprises, what with the tour to Mount Myohyang looming ahead again.

We were wrong, however. Christian and Kay had been hanging around with the German television people from Moscow and through them had met a German emergency doctor by the name of Norbert Vollertsen. Vollertsen had been living in Pyongyang for a year-and-a-half, and knew much about the real situation in the country, having been active in hospitals outside the capital.

It was my last day in Pyongyang, and Vollertsen — a guy in his forties, tall, blonde and deeply tanned — was waiting for Christian, Kay and myself in the hotel bar. We simply sped off together in his

*English language media in both North and South Korea referred to prisoners as "unconverted". Of course, the South tried to "convert" the Commies into good citizens of the capitalist South...

white jeep, gangsta rap blaring from the speakers. "Where do you want to go?" Vollertsen asked. Without the official guides by our side, white-washing and hiding anything they didn't want us to see, Pyongyang suddenly felt transformed. Now we were able to get up close to the pyramid hotel, which was particularly ghastly, and travel to poor neigh-bourhoods, where the buildings might have been relatively new but of such shoddy quality that they were already close to collapse. Next we travelled to the quarters of the local high officials, mansions that could proudly stand alongside Lac Leman's finest, but off-limits to regular people. We drove by many large groups of children preparing for the gymnastics display for the Party anniversary. According to Vollertsen, the children trained like this for up to six hours a day, and still had their regular school work to deal with.

Christian wanted to ride the subway — without Miss Choe or Miss Pak watching over him. All right, said Vollertsen, no problem. We hopped onto the escalator and rode down far beneath the city. Pyongyang has

Old Berlin subway car
in Pyongyang.
Photo: Christian Karl

the deepest subway in the world — so deep in fact that it will suppos-edly provide shelter against nuclear attack. I was reiterating this fact to the others when suddenly Christian exclaimed, "Look who's here!" I turned around and couldn't believe what I saw: Miss Pak — right be-hind us! How did she get here?! She asked Christian the same thing. "We've got a new guide," I yelled over. "Don't worry."

Upon reaching the bottom of the escalator, she strongly urged us to turn around and travel back up again with her. No way. "Just jump onto the next train," Vollertsen whispered.

"Don't take a train!" Miss Pak implored us. "I have to meet some-one!"

"Don't worry," I repeated. "Go ahead with your meeting. We've got a new guide."

Of course, she jumped onto the train with us.

It was an old West Berlin train. The North Koreans had eliminated virtually every trace of its origins but there was no doubt about it — we knew Berlin trains. Pictures of Great Leaders one and two adorned every car, but the graffiti scratched into the windows by Berlin teenagers was still visible — to remove it would have meant replacing the glass. They don't even do that in Berlin. I felt suddenly at home and said that I wouldn't get off the train until it arrived at Kottbusser Tor. But we were on the wrong train. After one station, the ride was over — final station. We had to go back.

What to do now? We would get into serious trouble if we just ignored the fact that Miss Pak was with us — and she would get into trouble, too. We decided to return to the hotel with her and head out again later that night, prowling the dark streets one last time.

With revolutionary music playing softly inside the Air Koryo plane, I took out the bundle of papers that Dr Norbert Vollertsen had given to me — his reports to the headquarters of Cap Anamur, the aid organisation for which he worked.

A few short excerpts... In an entry dated December 2, 1999, Vollertsen had written:

December in Korea. The wind is bitingly cold. The drive to Haeju can only be undertaken slowly and very carefully. Crashed trucks all over the roadside remind one of the treacherousness of the icy roads. And people — more on the way now than on some days during the height of summer — walking, by bicycle, with luggage sometimes larger than the person carrying it. Thin jackets and head scarves serve as little protection from the cold. Frost in their hair, everybody looks powdered white. We would need a car capable of carrying thousands to pick up all the people standing on the roadside, waving with packs of cigarettes and begging for a lift. After hours of useless waiting, most of them lie down on the ground, utterly disillusioned — if they haven't already set the roadside slopes afire in order to get a little warmth. The hills around the towns and villages are barren. No trees in sight, every scrap of wood used to keep the fireplaces going. Winter in Korea. And this is just the beginning.

Outside the hospital in Chaerjong, the local 'ambulance' is waiting — an ox cart loaded with straw. On top of it a thin garish blanket. Underneath the blanket a horribly pale, emaciated woman, her face etched in pain. She was 'released' from treatment — because there is no medicine left. The aid supplies are urgently required but are still sat in Sinuiju, on the North Korean-Chinese border, awaiting transportation. Eighteen-hundred — maybe as many as 2,500 — train cars are just sitting there, most of them carrying aid supplies from a variety of aid organisations, ours amongst them. Almost all are labelled 'high priority shipments' — particularly those containing complete sets of furniture and cases of red wine for the officials of the numerous aid organisation at their 'deprived outposts'. As with the red wine, the infusion medicines will suffer from the frost. One has only to explain this to the North Korean railway authority — and then track down the right train cars, secure electricity or diesel oil, hope for the best...

The worst however is this: nobody believes in the future anymore. In the hospitals, the pipes of the original central heating systems have been ripped out and are being used to hold up the plastic sheets in the green houses. In place of the old heating system, holes are punched into walls adjoining primitive outdoor stoves, in order to allow at least a little warmth into the rooms. Buckets take the place of taps, filled with water from improvised wells. The water pipes have been ripped out and used as support material elsewhere. Nobody believes that the old city water-supply system will ever work again. Everywhere else in the world progress is being made, but here things slip backwards into the stone age — the hand-made axes of that era can already be seen occasionally here...

Beijing. Reconnecting to the 'real world'. My walk to the closest Internet café is much shorter than last year, one having since opened on Tiananmen Square, a stone's throw from the Mao mausoleum.

Many thanks to Dr Norbert Vollertsen, who was expelled from North Korea at the end of 2000 for exposing too many of the country's dirty secrets to the Western press. He now resides in Seoul where he campaigns for the improvement of human rights in North Korea.

Nicolas Righetti would eventually publish a photo book about North Korea — Le Dernier Paradise *(pub: Edition Olisane, Genève, 2002) — that didn't simply feature tourist snaps. Of course he could never admit that this had been his intention while being interrogated...*

His fifty-minute video documentary, Guided Tour in North Korea, *had its world premiere at the Calcutta Film Festival in spring 2002.*

Index of Film Titles

NEW BOOKS FROM CRITICAL VISION

"A vastly
intriguing book"

John Keel

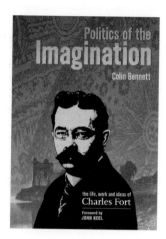

*Available
May 2002*

POLITICS OF THE IMAGINATION

The Life, Work and Ideas of Charles Fort

by Colin Bennett

Born in Albany, New York, in 1874, Charles Fort spent almost his entire life searching through periodicals in the New York Public Library and the British Museum, compiling evidence to show that science was a mere façade which concealed as much as it claimed to have discovered. In a series of four books — *The Book of the Damned, New Lands, Lo!* and *Wild Talents* — he argued that explanations are far more fantastic than the things they are supposed to explain, and that we only use them to get some sleep at night. Science, believed Fort, was a new form of social control whose object was to conceal the fantastical nature of the universe by means of editing out paradoxes, contradictions, miracles, paranormal events—anything that was unusual or which did not fit into a set scheme of things.

The "foe of science" is how the *New York Times* described Fort in its obituary...

Politics of the Imagination has a foreword by the writer John Keel, whose book *The Mothman Prophecies* is now a major motion picture starring Richard Gere.

ISBN **1-900486-20-2**   Price UK **£12.99** / US **$19.95**   Pages **176pp**

Market **Biography / Forteana**   Publication **May, 2002**

www.headpress.com

"Some of the best bizarre film commentary going… with sharp, no-nonsense verdicts"

The Village Voice

Available Sept 2002

SLIMETIME

A Guide To Sleazy, Mindless Movies

by Steven Puchalski

Seriously warped movies from around the world! Sci-fi, schlock, women-in-prison, Japanese monsters, biker gangs, brazen gals, mindless men, kung fu mischief, bad music, flower power, and puppet people!

Utilising over in-depth reviews, cast and plot details, **Slimetime** wallows in those films which the world has deemed it best to forget — everything from cheesy no-budget exploitation to the embarrassing efforts of major studios.

Many of the motion pictures in slimetime have never seen a major release, some were big hits, others have simply 'vanished'. To compliment the wealth of reviews are detailed essays on specific sleaze genres such as Biker, Blaxploitation and Drug movies.

This fully updated & revised edition contains a hundred new reviews, many new illustrations and a striking cover.

ISBN **1-900486-21-0** Price UK **£14.99** / US **$19.95** Pages **224pp**

Market **Film & TV / Popular Culture** Publication **September 2002**

www.headpress.com

"Jack Stevenson is a brilliant fifth scholar —he's obsessive, funny, and knows more about obscure, dirty movies than anyone alive"
John Waters

Reprint available Dec 2002

FLESHPOT

Cinema's Sexual Myth Makers & Taboo Breakers

Jack Stevenson, Editor

Fleshpot is an indispensable guide to the outré realms of erotic cinema, a delirious sampling of the genres, personalities and trends that have set screens aflame since the dawn of motion pictures. From the pioneering 'Nudies' and 'Stags' to the American Pre-Code Talkies and the racy European imports of the Forties and Fifties — from soft-core to hard-core and beyond — Fleshpot probes beneath the façades of art, exploitation and underground film genres to reveal... sleaze!

For ten years Jack Stevenson has been writing and collating materials on the history and lore of sex cinema. **Fleshpot**, a compendium of texts by an international group of experts and cult film personalities (including Kenneth Anger and George Kuchar), is the result. Illustrated throughout, **Fleshpot** is a fascinating and informative introduction to some of cinema's most notable sexual myth makers and taboo breakers.

ISBN **1-900486-12-1**   Price UK **£14.95** / US **$19.95**   Pages **256 pp**

Market **Cinema / Cult Film**   Reprinted **December 2002**

www.headpress.com

Available Jan 2003

LAND OF A 1000 BALCONIES

Discoveries and Confessions of a B-movie Archaeologist

by Jack Stevenson

Most books about B-movies are straightforward genre guides, biographies or encyclopaedias. Not this one. In addition to meticulously researched chapters on film showmen, gimmicks and cult films, *Land of a 1000 Balconies* documents author Jack Stevenson's first-hand exploration of a different realm of low-budget cinema…

Amongst these explorations are film-related incidents and episodes, character-studies and reports of unusual film happenings, all of which the author has — over the past fifteen years — been privy or party to in his various capacities as show organiser, tour arranger, festival jury member and 16mm projectionist-for-hire in both Europe and the US.

Elsewhere Stevenson focuses on movie theatres and renegade exhibition spaces, as well as lamenting on the disappearing 'sense of place' and atmosphere that is such an integral part of the movie-going experience. Here the reader is invited to tour a diversity of venues—from the notorious old grindhouses of San Francisco's Market Street, through the home-made store-front cinemas of Seattle and New York, to the underground film clubs of Europe.

ISBN **1-900486-23-7**   Price UK **£14.99** / US **$19.95**   Pages **224pp**

Market **Film & TV / Popular Culture**   Publication **January 2003**

www.headpress.com

NEW BOOKS FROM CRITICAL VISION

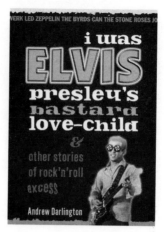

NEW BOOKS FROM CRITICAL VISION

"The best peep-
show coverage of
the porn-video
business"

Screw

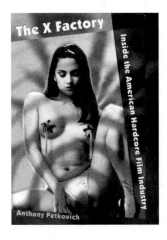

*Available
Now*

THE X FACTORY

Inside the American Hardcore Film Industry

by Anthony Petkovich

AT LAST! BACK IN PRINT! Since 1972 and the release of *Deep Throat*, the business of making commercial hardcore feature films has grown dramatically. Thousands of films are produced every year. Yet for the most part the industry remains a mysterious commodity, with the people behind it still seen as unscrupulous, vaguely threatening figures.

Much has been written about the porn film industry, some of it by those vehemently opposed to it, some of it kiss-and-tell by those once part of it. Now the record is put straight by the people who are a part of that industry today. **The X Factory** is an eye-opening trip into adult feature films.

This reprint has eight new pages in full-colour.

ISBN **1-900486-24-5** Price UK **£14.99** / US **$19.95** Pages **208pp**

Market **Film**   Publication **Available Now**

www.headpress.com

NEW BOOKS FROM CRITICAL VISION

"HEADPRESS RULES!"

Spectator

Available Now

HEADPRESS *The journal of sex religion death*

23: FUNHOUSE

David Kerekes, Editor

CULT FILM SPECIAL! This twenty-third edition of **Headpress** is devoted to seventies horror classic **Last House on Dead End Street**, a visceral cult obscurity inspired by the Manson murders and fuelled by the copious intake of drugs.

We track down the reclusive director, Roger Watkins, several of the film's stars, and also cast on eye over Watkins' post-**Last House** career in the porn business.

ISBN **1-900486-18-0**   ISSN **1353-9760**   Price UK **£8.99** / US **$14.99**

Pages **176pp**   Market **Pop Culture**   Published **Available Now**